IT HAPPENED IN TEXAS

To all of my writer friends in Texas.
Their numbers are legion.

CONTENTS

CONTENTS

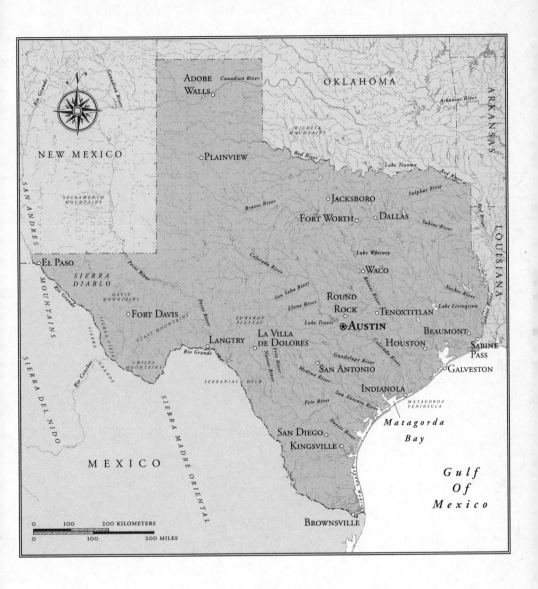

TEXAS

PREFACE

This book highlights several interesting episodes of Texas history from the days of the prehistoric Indians through modern times. Each story is complete in itself and can be read individually and out of sequence.

Texas is an extremely important state historically, and although the vignettes related in this book do not in any way purport to be a thorough history of the state, they have been chosen selectively to give the reader a broad understanding of the varied historical background of the "Lone Star State."

I hope that *It Happened in Texas* will provide a few hours of pleasure to those who read it, and that it will, perhaps, find its way into the classrooms of the state, thereby giving younger generations a better appreciation of their vast heritage.

A PREHISTORIC HUNT
IN THE PANHANDLE

- 5900 B.C. -

THE BAND NUMBERED NO MORE THAN THREE OR four dozen people, mostly men and women, but a small group of older children tagged along as well. The younger tots had been left behind with a few women at a temporary campsite near a stream two miles away. The day was warm and dry, typical of late summer on the northwestern Texas plains. But to the men and women of the group, the weather was immaterial, for today they hunted bison. Everyone knew that before the sun vanished in the western sky, the band would have a large part of the meat and hides necessary to feed and clothe them during the coming winter.

The people were not native to these environs. They had marched across the dry prairie from the northeast, specifically to hunt bison. They called no place home but rather moved about constantly, following the great game animals that provided them with food and materials for shelter.

The horse, although originally native to North America, had already become extinct there and had not yet been reintroduced by Europeans. Consequently, these people, members of a cultural group archaeologists call "Paleo," traveled on foot accompanied only by their ever-present dogs. They were armed with spears and skinning knives rather than bows and arrows, which were not yet in use in North America.

On the previous day, a pair of scouts had brought news of the bison's approach. The excited men had run into the small camp and hastily told their leaders that a herd of almost one hundred animals was traveling in a straight line toward their camp. They had left it about twenty miles away, and they figured that by about noon tomorrow, the animals—larger than bison of today—would be nearing the little creek that flowed nearby. The hunters knew from experience that the great shaggy beasts would spend the day drinking from the stream, one of the few sources of fresh water for miles around.

The scouts also brought news of their discovery, about two miles upstream from camp, of a broad draw that led from the elevated plain to the brink of a deep gully. The draw would make an ideal place through which to stampede the herd over the edge of the precipice. Then hunters could jump in and kill them. The prospect of killing so many bison at one time excited the members of the band. They knew that if they were successful, the day's harvest of fresh meat would exceed by many times that acquired during a typical hunt.

It was about noon when the hunters saw a cloud of dust on the horizon that told them the bison herd was approaching. Scattering about the head of the draw, the men, women, and children found hiding places behind clumps of tall prairie grass and waited. Fate was with them, for the wind was right, blowing toward them from the direction of their prey.

Soon the hunters heard a rumbling from afar. The earth shook, and the animals, sensing the presence of water, came faster. The bison made a beeline for the stream, and as they passed through the draw, they panicked as the men, women, and children rose from their hiding places. Shouting and waving buffalo robes, the people herded all of the bison in the direction of the precipice.

As the lead animals approached the gully, they did not notice that they were about to step off into empty space until it was too late. The bison behind them frantically pushed them over the edge before joining them in a mass of broken bones and bleeding bodies. More hunters, concealed along the walls of the draw, finished off the terrified bison one by one with their spears. The entire episode was over within minutes.

It was a good hunt. Nearly all of the one hundred animals lay dead. By day's end, the women would skin and butcher most of them, leaving untouched the few animals that were first to go over the edge, since they had been crushed under the sheer weight of the more recent casualties.

Archaeologists estimate that this ancient bison kill, which occurred nearly eight thousand years ago in what is now the Texas Panhandle, yielded hundreds of pounds of meat, fat, and organs, plus scores of hides. And if these prehistoric people were anything like the Plains Indians of more recent times, they also made use of many of the bones, ligaments, and other body parts of the versatile animal.

While the details of this hunting sequence comprise an archaeologist's best guess, the site itself is beyond dispute. In 1944 highway workers near Plainview discovered it while excavating for road-building materials. Scientists from the Texas Memorial Museum were immediately called in, and during the next year they found the remains of the one hundred or so slaughtered bison. Unique spear points were still embedded in the bones of some of the animals. Archaeologists dubbed them "Plainview points," after the nearby town. Helen M. Wormington, an archaeologist who wrote extensively on early people in North America, later observed that it was the association of extinct animal remains with projectile points that gave this site such great archaeological significance.

Even before the Plainview site was discovered, spear points with strong Plainview characteristics had been found all over North America, from Alaska to Mexico and from Florida to Ontario. But it is the site in Texas that gave the distinctive style its name.

A TREK ACROSS TEXAS

- A.D. 1534 -

ON A HOT SUMMER DAY IN 1534 in what is now southern Texas, Álvar Núñez Cabeza de Vaca crouched over a young man with a serious chest wound. For the past six years, Cabeza de Vaca, a high-ranking Spanish official, had been the captive of Gulf Coast Indians. But he had earned the trust of his captors, and they perceived him as a powerful medicine man.

The youth before him now had been injured during a skirmish with a neighboring tribe. Part of an arrow protruded from his chest, and Cabeza de Vaca realized that the stone point might be lodged near the boy's heart. Although his knowledge of human anatomy was limited, the Spaniard knew his patient could die if not treated immediately.

Six years of living in the wilderness had taught Cabeza de Vaca well. He had become proficient at making knives from flint, taking care to hone each blade to a razor-sharp edge. With one of these, he began to explore the young warrior's wound. He dug into the flesh, trying not to cause extensive bleeding. The pain must have been excruciating, but the Indian endured the procedure well. Cabeza de Vaca ordered a spectator to find him some thin deer sinew, and he quickly sewed the gaping wound closed. To the Spaniard's relief, the lad lived to fight again.

Although Cabeza de Vaca possessed no medical degree, he might be called the first white physician ever to practice in Texas. He had come to America in 1528 to serve as treasurer of Pánfilo de Narváez's Florida expedition. A storm had shipwrecked the explorers, but Cabeza de Vaca and some companions managed to build a few crude boats and set sail again, only to be shipwrecked a second time somewhere near what is now Galveston Island. This time, the survivors were captured by Karankawa Indians and put to work as slaves.

For eight years, Cabeza de Vaca lived among the Karankawas and other tribes who lived in the region. Survival was not easy. One of his fellow captives later wrote that they were "used more cruelly than by a Moor, naked and barefoot on a coast that burns like fire in summer."

However, in time, Cabeza de Vaca won his captors' trust and was able to move freely among them. He later wrote that he

> set to trafficking, and strove to make my employment profitable in the ways I could best contrive, and by that means I got food and good treatment. . . . With my merchandise and trade I went into the interior as far as I pleased, and traveled along the coast forty or fifty leagues. . . . This occupation suited me well; for the travel allowed me the liberty to go where I wished, I was not obliged to work, and was not a slave.

For reasons not entirely known today, Cabeza de Vaca's captors assumed he was a competent medicine man. He realized that he did sometimes have luck curing various maladies of the native population, so he wisely took advantage of his healing skills. He soon discovered that he could obtain special favors from the Indians if he carefully acted out the role of medicine man. Some tribesmen came to revere him highly, although he was still considered a prisoner.

Years later, when Cabeza de Vaca wrote of his captivity, he said he became a healer because the natives "wished to make us physicians, without examination or inquiring for diplomas." Aware that his life depended upon whether he cured the sick, Cabeza de Vaca continuously called upon Divine Providence to assist him in his work. He later wrote:

> Our method was to bless the sick, breathing upon them
> and recite a Pater-noster and an Ave Maria, praying
> with all earnestness to God our Lord that He would
> give health and influence them to make us some good
> return. In His clemency He willed that all those for
> whom we supplicated should tell the others that they
> were sound and in health, directly after we made the
> sign of the blessed cross over them. For this the Indians
> treated us kindly; they deprived themselves of food that
> they might give to us, and presented us with skins and
> some trifles.

Cabeza de Vaca's eight-year trek across southern Texas has been described as one of the most spectacular journeys ever undertaken by a human being. Dirty, sunburned, never knowing what indignities lay ahead, he was swapped from tribe to tribe, yet he survived. Later he noted that he and his companions often were forced to go naked and

> *twice a year we cast our skins like serpents. The sun and*
> *air produced great sores on our breasts and shoulders,*
> *giving us sharp pain; and the large load we had [to*
> *carry] . . . caused the cords to cut into our arms. . . .*
> *The country is so broken and thickly set, that . . .*
> *thorns and shrubs tore our flesh wherever we went.*

Cabeza de Vaca always traveled with one thought in mind—to get to the Spanish settlements in Mexico, which he thought were somewhere to the west. In 1536, he and a few companions reached safety there. Everyone stared at the wild-looking men who could hardly speak their native tongue anymore. But one of Cabeza de Vaca's companions, a black Moor named Estevanaco, told the wide-eyed conquistadors just what they wanted to hear—that a wonderful land of gold, silver, and other fabulous riches lay to the northeast. It was a tale that Spanish explorer Francisco Vásquez de Coronado would one day discover the hard way was nothing but a lie.

THE MURDER OF LA SALLE

- 1687 -

RENÉ ROBERT CAVELIER, SIEUR DE LA SALLE, LOOKED LONGINGLY out the gate of the makeshift post that he had built in what is now East Texas. It was January 7, 1687, and the French explorer and several of his followers were about to leave the place they called Fort Saint Louis to begin a long overland journey. They hoped it would take them to the Illinois country and eventually to Canada.

La Salle and his men had sailed from France aboard several ships and landed at Matagorda Bay in 1685. They thought they had reached the mouth of the Mississippi River, which La Salle had discovered on a previous expedition in 1682. A few days later when his ship, the *Aimable,* was wrecked off the Gulf Coast, La Salle and about three dozen followers found themselves lost in the wilderness.

The stranded Frenchmen eventually realized that they were nowhere near the Mississippi. They built Fort Saint Louis to protect themselves from the elements and the Indians who lived in the neighborhood. Several attempts to find the Mississippi failed, and

La Salle decided to try one more time to escape from this unfamiliar land.

As the party of seventeen men and five horses passed through the gates of Fort Saint Louis, the twenty people who would remain gathered to wish them farewell. With La Salle was his older brother, who was a priest, two nephews, several soldiers, a friar, a surgeon, and a couple of Indian guides and hunters. Historian Francis Parkman described the beginning of the journey in great detail in his classic book, *La Salle and the Discovery of the Great West:*

> *It was a bitter parting, one of sighs, tears, and embracings,—the farewell of those on whose souls had sunk a heavy boding that they would never meet again. Equipped and weaponed for the journey, the adventurers filed from the gate, crossed the river, and held their slow march over the prairies beyond, till intervening woods and hills shut Fort St. Louis forever from their sight.*
>
> *The travelers . . . wore the remains of the clothing they had worn from France, eked out with deer-skins, dressed in the Indian manner; and some had coats of old sail-cloth. . . . They suffered greatly from the want of shoes, and found for a while no better substitute than a casing of raw buffalo hide, which they were forced to keep always wet, as, when dry, it hardened about the foot like iron. At length they bought dressed deer-skin from the Indians, of which they made tolerable moccasins. . . . At night, they usually set a rude*

stockade about their camp; and here, by the grassy bor-
der of a brook, or at the edge of a grove where a spring
bubbled up through the sands, they lay asleep around
the embers of their fire, while the man on guard lis-
tened to the deep breathing of the slumbering horses,
and the howling of the wolves.

When La Salle's party was a little more than two months out of
Fort Saint Louis, wandering aimlessly through the region that lies
northwest of today's city of Houston, the Frenchman began to worry.
Several of his men had failed to return from a scouting party. (As it
turned out, three of them, including one of La Salle's nephews, had
been murdered by the others.) La Salle decided to look for them the
following day. Accompanied by the friar and an Indian scout, he set
out on March 19, 1687. The friar later wrote of the Frenchman's
temperament during the journey:

All the way, he spoke to me of nothing but matters of
piety, grace, and predestination; enlarging on the debt
he owed to God, who had saved him from so many
perils during more than twenty years of travel in Amer-
ica. Suddenly, I saw him overwhelmed with a pro-
found sadness, for which he himself could not account.
He was so much moved that I scarcely knew him.

As La Salle and his companions continued on their journey, they
noticed a pair of eagles flying high above them. Believing that the
missing men's camp was probably nearby, La Salle fired a shot into
the air. When one of the missing men followed the sound to reach

them, La Salle asked where his nephew and the others were. According to Parkman's account,

> *the man, without lifting his hat, or any show of respect, replied in an agitated and broken voice, but with a tone of studied insolence, that Moranget [the nephew] was strolling about somewhere. La Salle rebuked and menaced him. He rejoined with increased insolence, drawing back . . . while the incensed commander advanced to chastise him. At that moment a shot was fired from the grass, instantly followed by another; and, pierced through the brain, La Salle dropped dead. . . . The murderers now came forward, and with wild looks gathered about their victim. . . . With mockery and insult, they stripped it [the corpse] naked, dragged it into the bushes, and left it there, a prey to the buzzards and the wolves.*
>
> *Thus, in the vigor of his manhood, at the age of forty-three, died Robert Cavelier de la Salle . . . without question one of the most remarkable explorers whose names live in history.*

The perpetrators of the crime were La Salle's surgeon, Liotot, and a man named Duhaut. Apparently, both were frustrated by their leader's inability to rescue them from what they believed would be certain death in the wilderness of East Texas. The men's loss of patience cost France the life of the man who, only a few years earlier, had stood at the mouth of the Mississippi River and claimed its entire watershed for his king.

Later that year, La Salle's murderers were executed by other members of their party. The few remaining wanderers finally found their way to Arkansas Post, a small French fort at the mouth of the Arkansas River. The men left behind at Fort Saint Louis were killed by Indians or assimilated into their tribes.

THE MISLEADING MUSTANG HUNT

- 1801 -

AFTER WANDERING FOR FIVE MONTHS through the seemingly endless prairies of what is now Louisiana and East Texas, the two dozen or so men of Philip Nolan's command probably lost track of time. They knew it was spring, because the grasslands were beginning to show new growth, but they probably did not know the exact date: March 21, 1801. Most of the men felt much more time had passed since they had left family and friends back East to take part in a "mustang hunt."

Nolan and his followers were camped in a crude stockade beside a small tributary of the Brazos River about forty miles north of today's city of Waco. They had been there for a little over two months and had spent most of their time scouring the plains for herds of wild horses. Once they found a herd, the men would harass the animals continuously, depriving them of food, water, and sleep until the horses became so tired that the men easily could drive them into makeshift corrals.

"Mustanging" was a profitable business. There was a ready market for wild horses back in the United States. Most of the men with Nolan assumed he had come to Texas to make his fortune rounding up the animals. The Spanish government, which controlled the region, at first believed that as well. But Nolan had other business to attend to in Texas. The adventurous Irishman was a secret agent for General James Wilkinson, the commanding general of the U.S. Army. Wilkinson nursed a secret ambition to rule a vast southwestern empire, wrested away from the Spanish. Aaron Burr, former vice president of the United States, would one day join him in the scheme.

When Spanish authorities began to suspect Nolan's ulterior motive for visiting Texas, they rescinded his passport and ordered him never to return to Spanish territory. But Nolan was an adventurer, and the smell of danger only made his heart beat faster. Defiantly, he and his men had set out from the Walnut Hills (today's Vicksburg, Mississippi) in early November 1800 on what would prove to be Nolan's last journey.

Shortly before dawn on March 21, Nolan was awakened by the frantic neighing of horses in a nearby corral. Grabbing a rifle, he crawled out of his bedroll and left the stockade to see what was spooking the animals. He also sent a detail of five men to take care of the horses. In the distance, silhouetted against the morning sun, Nolan could see Spanish soldiers. He wheeled rapidly, returned to the stockade, and alerted the other men. Minutes passed and, to his chagrin, the five men he had dispatched did not return. Nolan knew they had been captured by the Spanish militiamen. Only twenty Americans remained to defend the stockade.

The Spanish commander at Nacogdoches, a Lieutenant Musquiz, was in charge of the militia unit that surrounded the stockade. The Americans produced a white flag, and Nolan rode out to meet with

Musquiz and his interpreter. The lieutenant told Nolan that he had come to arrest the mustang hunters.

But Nolan refused to surrender and raced back to the protection of his stockade—only to discover that two of his men had deserted to the Spanish. Now only eighteen men, including himself, faced the one hundred or more well-armed Spanish cavalrymen. As the sun continued to rise, someone fired the first shot, and the battle was on.

The Americans soon found themselves without a leader, for Nolan, as he hurried from man to man urging them to make every shot count, was the first casualty, mortally wounded in the head. One of the mustangers, a Tennessean named Peter Ellis Bean, described the dangerous predicament in which Nolan's men now found themselves:

In a few minutes after [Nolan's death] they began to fire grape-shot at us. . . . We returned their fire until about nine o'clock. We then had two men wounded and one killed [Nolan]. I told my companions we ought to charge on the cannon and take it, but the rest appeared unwilling. I told them it was at most but death; and if we stood still, all would doubtless be killed . . . we must take the cannon, or retreat. It was agreed that we should retreat.

Now only fifteen men were capable of fighting, and they decided to try to sneak out of the stockade and escape up a deep ravine. The Spanish interpreter caught up with them and persuaded them to surrender. After the Americans returned to the stockade, they buried Nolan, but only after Musquiz insisted on cutting off his ears so he could send them as a present to Governor Elguezabal of Texas.

The governor was elated. He sent a dispatch to the commanding general of the Spanish army at Chihuahua in which he said:

> *I forward to you the ears of that American, with all the papers found on his person, which should be examined and translated. Lieutenant Musquiz' success has been so fortunate, inasmuch as it was accomplished with no loss of lives in his party.*

Although Nolan's untimely death temporarily halted Wilkinson's "Spanish Conspiracy," it did not halt the general's continued interest in the scheme, which he pursued to no avail for the next several years. As for the captured Americans, most of them were eventually sent to Mexico as prisoners of the Crown, and several of them, including Peter Ellis Bean, spent years in Spanish prisons.

A FRENCH NATURALIST
MEETS THE INDIANS

- 1828 -

ON FEBRUARY 2, 1828, A SMALL PARTY of Mexican soldiers led by
thirty-seven-year-old General Manuel Mier y Terán—once described
by Stephen Austin as "the most scientific man who belongs to the
[Mexican] army"—crossed the Rio Grande from Mexico into Texas.
Their mission was to define the boundary that separated the United
States from Mexico and to explore the vast region of Texas that lay
between San Antonio and Nacogdoches.

With General Mier y Terán was a twenty-year-old French natural-
ist by the name of Jean Louis Berlandier. The young scientist, who had
received his formal training in Switzerland, had come to Mexico in late
1826. A year later, when the Mexican congress appropriated fifteen
thousand pesos to fund the general's expedition, Berlandier eagerly vol-
unteered for the mission. Also traveling with the expedition was Lieutenant Jose María Sánchez y Tapia, a brilliant artist and topographer
who would capture in a series of watercolors the traditional cultures of

many of the Texas Indians. Berlandier later wrote a book about his travels, and in it he described the tribes with which the expedition came in contact, among them the Lipan Apaches and the Comanches.

After crossing the Rio Grande in early February, Mier y Terán and his party stayed in Laredo for nearly three weeks, giving Berlandier the opportunity to visit nearby villages and study the region's plant life. While in Laredo, expedition members were visited by a war party of Lipan Apaches, who made a bad first impression on Berlandier. Of them, he wrote:

> The Lipans have no desire to devote themselves to the arts of farming, although they have already shown that they are at least as gifted at agriculture as they are for the nomadic life. Corrupted by now through their dealings with the villages, and all too eager to steal and to plunder, they refuse to submit to the responsibilities society imposes on all of us. Like the lower classes in the great cities, the Lipans reap where they have not sown and steal livestock they have not raised. To this occupation they devote a zeal and perseverance deplored by the inhabitants of the lands they range. . . .
>
> The Lipans . . . engage in at least a little trade. They come to the presidios in caravans of several hundred, provided they are at peace with the garrison, to sell their buffalo hides (covered with painting), bear grease, smoked and dried meat, and above all, furs. In the single presidio of Nacogdoches, the natives sell . . . deerskins and beaver skins, not to mention the hides of buffalo and bearskins.

By early March, the expedition had reached San Antonio, a village of about fifteen hundred people. During a stay in the mission town, Berlandier became acquainted with another large and important tribe of Texas Indians: the Comanches. Mexican relations with the Comanches were precarious, and Berlandier wrote:

> *When the Comanches . . . are . . . at war against the*
> *whole chain of [Mexican] presidios, and have no place*
> *to trade, they deal in the same goods with American*
> *traders, who bring their merchandise right into the*
> *rancherias, and who get from them not only the furs*
> *they have to sell, but also the mules and horses they*
> *have stolen from the townspeople with whom they are*
> *at war. . . . This trade, in which the inhabitants of*
> *both sides of the borders had engaged, has dropped off*
> *recently, since a few of these traders were killed a few*
> *years ago by some Comanches . . . whose rancherias*
> *they had visited.*

While among the Comanches, Berlandier got his first taste of broiled skunk. Once he got over his initial squeamishness, he decided that it was quite tasty. It reminded him of broiled pig.

Mier y Terán and his exploring party traveled as far as Nacogdoches before they turned around and headed back to Mexico. Back in the San Antonio region by fall, the men were invited to hunt buffalo with a group of Comanche braves, an activity that took them as far west as the headwaters of the Guadalupe River. Later in the year and during part of the next, Berlandier visited Goliad and Aransas Bay and traveled along the Gulf Coast as far as New Orleans and back again. The expedition returned to Matamoros in August 1829.

With the exception of a brief trip to San Antonio in 1834, Berlandier apparently never traveled to Texas again. Although he published some of his findings in Mexico as early as 1832, his name and contributions were ignored in the United States until 1852, when the Smithsonian Institution acquired part of his vast natural history collection. Over the years, Yale, Harvard, the Library of Congress, and the Thomas Gilcrease Institute of American History and Art in Tulsa, Oklahoma, also procured parts of the collection.

Jean Louis Berlandier's account of his travels in Texas is considered one of the most valuable scientific records of the United States. His biographer, John C. Ewers, called him "one of the most prolific and versatile writers on the American West prior to the extensive railway and Mexican boundary surveys in the 1850s." There can be little doubt that the young Frenchman's descriptions of the Indian tribes of Texas—and the watercolor paintings by Lieutenant Sánchez—rank with those of George Catlin, Prince Maximilian, and other better-known chroniclers of the same period.

CONSTRUCTION OF
AN EARLY CAPITAL

- 1830 -

ON JUNE 25, 1830, LIEUTENANT COLONEL FRANCISCO RUIZ set out from Bexar, Texas, with a sizable expedition consisting of one hundred men and an oxcart full of supplies. Ruiz's destination was the crossing of the Brazos River in present-day Burleson County, on the road that connected Bexar with Nacogdoches. His mission, which the Spanish general Manuel Mier y Terán had defined for him the previous April, was to build a fort at the river crossing to deter the immigration of Americans into the Mexican states of Coahuila and Texas.

On July 13, Ruiz and his command reached the Brazos River and began to build a temporary post about half a mile downstream from the crossing. The lieutenant colonel must have wondered how this tiny fort in the wilderness, one of several that General Mier y Terán had ordered built, was going to stop the flood of Americans that had been pouring into Texas since 1821. Three days after Ruiz's arrival at the site, the general referred to the place as "Tenoxtitlan," after the Aztec capital of the same name.

The fort also was needed to house troops who would escort military payroll money from Bexar to Nacogdoches. In July, Mier y Terán hinted at the significance of the fort when he wrote to his secretary of state:

> *It is extremely important that it be settled in order to keep Texas in subjection, and it is very well suited for Mexican colonists because the land is adequate for farming and ranching. . . . In my opinion this point, if it is developed, will in time become the capital of all Texas.*

As soon as Ruiz completed the temporary fort on the banks of the Brazos, he set about finding a more satisfactory, permanent location for the post. His choice was a plot "six leagues to the west of the Upper Crossing of the Brazos River," or several miles upstream from the temporary stockade. Although General Mier y Terán had originally ordered the post to be constructed of stone, the absence of that resource in the area eliminated the option. Ruiz used timber cut from the river bottom instead. Trees and underbrush were removed for a distance of eleven hundred feet from all sides of the fort so that its defenders could see approaching enemies and fire on them effectively. Finally, on October 17, 1830, the small garrison at Tenoxtitlan moved into its permanent home.

About a week after occupying the new fort, Ruiz was informed that a small group of Americans had approached the post and requested an audience with him. They were led by Sterling C. Robertson, a Tennessean, who produced official papers showing that he had been granted several thousand acres of nearby land for the establishment of a colony. Robertson had formed his organization, called the Nashville Company, in light of Mexico's previously lenient immigration laws. Now the Tennessean and his companions were ready to take up residence on their land in the Brazos River valley. Robertson told Ruiz that about fifty more followers were camped just a few miles away, waiting for the signal to proceed.

Ruiz was faced with a dilemma. His very reason for being stationed here on the frontier was to prohibit Americans from entering Texas. But these Americans clearly had a legitimate claim. He had seen the documents. He expressed his ambivalence on paper a few months later when he wrote to Stephen Austin, "I cannot help seeing the advantages which, to my way of thinking, would result if we admitted honest, hard-working people, regardless of what country they come from . . . even hell itself."

But Ruiz realized that he had no authority to allow the Americans to settle in the area he had been sent to protect. He fired letters to Matamoros and Leona Vicario (today's Saltillo), requesting advice on how to handle the ticklish situation. In the meantime, the soldiers of Fort Tenoxtitlan and the Tennesseans became good friends, particularly after the Nashville Company's physician, Dr. Thomas J. Wootton, treated the Mexicans' various maladies free of charge.

Three months later, Ruiz received the replies he had been dreading. His superiors told him to "give orders to the effect that neither Sterling Robertson nor any other North American family shall be allowed to settle in Tenoxtitlan." They went on to tell Ruiz to turn the Robertson party over to the military commandant of Nacogdoches "so that he may transport them without fail to the other side of the Sabine."

Ruiz tried to buy time by notifying his superiors that Robertson and his followers had left the area. Indeed, after a brief rest at Fort

Tenoxtitlan, the Americans moved on to other parts of Texas. Much to his relief, Ruiz was spared the embarrassment of having to take his new friends captive.

Tenoxtitlan was not destined to become the capital of Texas as Mier y Terán had predicted. Instead, the small community of Waterloo, later renamed Austin, was tapped for that honor in 1839. Fort Tenoxtitlan was abandoned in August 1832, and soon afterward the region was overrun by American immigrants. After a particularly fierce Indian raid in 1841, the village surrounding the fort ceased to exist.

THE FALL OF THE ALAMO

- 1836 -

Lieutenant Colonel William Barrett Travis dropped his raw-boned frame into a wobbly chair next to the rough-hewn table in his quarters. It was Wednesday, February 24, 1836, and for the past day, about one thousand Mexican soldiers had been pounding with artillery and small-arms fire at the old Spanish mission in San Antonio called the Alamo. Travis had carried a tremendous burden since the loss of his co-commander, Jim Bowie, to a severe illness. Now he was the sole leader of about two hundred American and European defenders holed up inside the mission.

Travis was at his wit's end. How in God's name could he be expected to lead his men to victory with the odds stacked against him in such proportions? The men were getting jittery waiting for the Mexicans to attack. Something had to be done, and it had to be done fast.

Travis laid a piece of yellowed paper on the table before him. He pulled an oil lamp closer and watched as long shadows danced on the walls of the darkened room. Retrieving a pen and inkwell from a nearby shelf, he began to write:

Fellow Citizens and Compatriots: I am besieged with a thousand or more of the Mexicans under Santa Anna. I have sustained a continual Bombardment and cannonade for 24 hours and have not lost a man. The enemy has demanded a surrender at discretion, otherwise, the garrison are to be put to the sword, if the fort is taken. I have answered the demand with a cannon shot, and our flag still waves proudly from the wall. I shall never surrender or retreat. Then, I call on you in the name of Liberty, of patriotism and everything dear to the American character, to come to our aid with all dispatch. The enemy is receiving reinforcements daily and will no doubt increase to three or four thousand in four or five days. If this call is neglected, I am determined to sustain myself as long as possible and die like a soldier who never forgets what is due his honor or that of his country. VICTORY or DEATH.

Travis replaced the pen in its stand, pushed himself away from the table, and stood up. Folding the letter neatly, he strode to the door and summoned a courier. Travis placed the note in the man's hand, stressed the importance of getting through the enemy lines, and wished him Godspeed. The man stepped back, saluted, and in a flash, mounted a horse and passed through the gates of the mission.

In the next few days, all of Travis's fears were realized. Even as he wrote his plea for assistance, General Antonio López de Santa Anna's forces outside the walls of the mission were being reinforced by an additional regiment of cavalry and three battalions of infantry. However, when a few brave Mexicans crept up to within a hundred or so yards of the Alamo, Travis's sharpshooters picked them off.

On February 27, other messengers were dispatched from the Alamo with orders to ride to Goliad, about eighty-five miles to the southeast. There, Colonel James Fannin had assembled four hundred fighters, but he was having troubles of his own and refused to send help to Travis. On February 29, Captain Juan Seguín, the commander of a small Mexican-American contingent at the Alamo, left the fortress to present Travis's plea to Fannin again, but he was met on the way by a messenger who told him that no help was forthcoming.

On March 3, Travis wrote another letter, his last one. He hoped that the courier would get through the enemy lines successfully to deliver the message to delegates at Washington-on-the-Brazos, 150 miles away. In his final plea, Travis wrote:

> *I look to the colonies alone for aid; unless it arrives*
> *soon I shall have to fight the enemy on his own terms. I*
> *will, however, do the best I can . . . and although we*
> *may be sacrificed . . . the victory will cost the enemy so*
> *dear, that it will be worse for him than defeat. I hope*
> *your honorable body will hasten reinforcements. . . .*
> *Our supply of ammunition is limited. . . . God and*
> *Texas. Victory or Death.*

As darkness approached on March 5, the Mexican cannons and small-arms fire ceased. The eerie silence worried the tired men inside the Alamo, who for the past several days had been constantly on the alert for an attack. A few defenders caught some badly needed sleep, while others stood guard.

At a few minutes past four o'clock on the morning of March 6, the Mexicans launched their final assault. In the dim light of the moon, four thousand of Santa Anna's troopers charged the Alamo. The mission's defenders pushed the attackers back twice, losing only a few men but much of their energy and ammunition. At eight o'clock, the Mexican army again attempted to breach the Alamo's walls. This time, with the help of scaling ladders, it succeeded.

Once inside, with orders from Santa Anna to fight to the death if necessary, the Mexicans slowly made their way through the grounds and buildings of the mission, killing all the defenders as they went. Within less than an hour, it was over, and the gallant men of the Alamo lay dead before Santa Anna. When Mexican commanders counted their casualties, they found that they had lost eight soldiers for every one defender.

In recent years, new research about the deadly action at the Alamo suggests that some of the Americans and Europeans inside may not have been killed in combat, but rather captured and executed later. Former Tennessee congressman and legendary frontiersman Davy Crockett is one of those who, according to the new evidence, met his fate in this manner. But there are many opponents to this myth-shattering idea. In some scholarly circles, the diary of the Mexican army officer who made these claims has been declared a forgery.

Regardless of how the brave men at the Alamo died, the fact remains that the event was one of the most one-sided battles in history. The Alamo's defenders went down—whether captured first or not—in a blaze of valor seldom encountered in the annals of military history.

AN ENGLISHWOMAN'S
COMANCHE BONDAGE

- 1836 -

SARAH ANN NEWTON HORN WAS BATHING THE INFANT of her sick friend, Mrs. Harris, when a band of about fifty Comanches rode into their makeshift camp. Along with her husband, John, and two small sons, Sarah Ann was on her way to Matamoros, Mexico. From there, the family intended to embark on the long journey home to their native England. They had become disenchanted with this dry, lonely part of Texas, a place that had been described so glowingly in the colonization literature published by John Charles Beales, an English physician.

Beales had recently arranged for several American and European families to settle on a large tract of land a few miles southwest of San Antonio. He had high hopes for his colony to become the shining example of the anglicization of Mexican Texas. But when the parched countryside failed to produce a single significant harvest, the Horns and several other colonists decided to return to England.

The small party had been traveling for nearly a month, after leaving the tiny settlement of La Villa de Dolores, near the headwaters of the Nueces River. Progress had been slow because the travelers were trying to avoid General Santa Anna and his Mexican army, which only recently, unbeknown to them, had annihilated the Texas garrison at the Alamo.

As the Comanches approached the colonists' camp, John Horn and his boys were admiring a homemade alligator-tooth necklace. Mrs. Harris, though ill, was managing to pick a few wild berries. Sarah Ann dried the Harris child and moved to her husband's side. She didn't like the looks of the Indians, she told him, but just as he began to reply, one of the Comanches killed him with an arrow. The other men in the party, surprised and unable to arm themselves, were cut down just as quickly. When the brief encounter was over, Sarah Ann scanned the bloody landscape and found that only she, Mrs. Harris, and the three children had survived. The Indians ransacked the wagons and then led the terrified women and children to a Comanche camp several miles away.

The survivors' first night with their Comanche captors gave them a taste of things to come. Sarah Ann later wrote that

> the Indians commenced stripping us of our bonnets,
> handkerchiefs, combs, and rings. They took everything
> from my children, leaving them as naked as they were
> born. . . . Mrs. Harris and myself were bound by pass-
> ing a cord about our ancles [sic] and arms, so as to
> bring the latter close to our sides. In this condition we
> were placed upon the naked ground, with a blanket
> thrown over us, and the whole of that dreadful night,
> my agonized heart seemed ready to burst, as I listened

to the cries of my orphan babes, as they called for their
murdered father, and for water to quench their thirst.

The next morning, the Comanches killed the Harris infant. Then they broke camp and set out across the plains. After traveling only a short distance, the women and their captors came across Mr. Harris and a young German, both of whom had been wounded and captured the previous day. Sarah Ann later recalled that

they were surrounded by a party of Indians who had
brought them in, and who had deferred killing them,
till, with true savage cruelty, they could torture us with
the sight. Mr. H. had a handkerchief bound about his
head. As we rode up, he cast an agonizing look at his
dear wife and myself, but he uttered not a word. As
soon as the company came to a halt, they were very
particular that we should look on while they shot them
both dead upon the spot.

The warm spring days turned into exhaustingly hot summer ones. On and on across the endless prairie, the Comanches and their band of captives traveled. Sarah Ann and her two sons were separated much of the time, and she could only imagine what torment the two little boys must be going through. One young Indian woman "was the unceasing tormentor of Mrs. H[arris] by night and day," Sarah Ann later recounted. Though small in stature, the woman took Mrs. Harris by the throat "and choked her, until the poor unresisting creature would turn black in the face, and fall as if dead at her feet; and then, to finish the tragedy, her cruel master would jump on her . . . and stamp her, until I have thought her sufferings were at an end."

In the following months, Sarah Ann was allowed to see her sons from time to time, but since they had been split up among different bands of Comanches, the visits were rare. Sarah Ann was treated as a slave and expected to perform any and all tasks demanded of her.

In late June 1837, some Spanish-Mexican traders, or comancheros, purchased Mrs. Harris from the Comanches and attempted unsuccessfully to buy Sarah Ann as well. At about the same time, the Indians terminated Sarah Ann's visits with her sons. She was now "a lonely exile," she wrote later, adding that

> *in the bonds of savage slavery, haunted by night and*
> *day with the image of my slaughtered husband, and*
> *tortured continually with an undying solicitude for my*
> *dear little ones, my life was little more than a scene of*
> *unmitigated misery; and the God of heaven only knows*
> *why, and how it is, that I am still alive!*

About three months later, near the village of San Miguel, New Mexico, the Comanches sold Sarah Ann to a wealthy American who treated her almost as badly as the Indians had. Eventually she was rescued by two Santa Fe traders operating under the instructions of William Donoho, who owned a hotel on the Santa Fe plaza. Sarah Ann learned that one of her sons had died and that the Comanches would not release the other for any price. Devastated by this news, she decided to flee to Missouri and then to England, where she could continue to crusade for her son's freedom.

But Sarah Ann Horn never saw England again. The physical abuse she had suffered at the hands of the Comanches, coupled with the distress she had experienced over the horrifying loss of her husband and children, finally took their toll. She died in New Franklin, Missouri, soon after she dictated a narrative describing her harrowing experiences as a captive of the Comanches.

THE TEXAN–SANTA FE EXPEDITION

- 1841 -

REPUBLIC OF TEXAS PRESIDENT MIRABEAU B. LAMAR HAD an idea. His infant country, still struggling for recognition, was burdened with $7 million in public debt—yet it had an annual income of less than half a million dollars. Lamar was confident that, in the three years since he had succeeded Sam Houston as president, he had brought Texas into the modern age by improving roads and expanding the school system. But he wanted to do more, and to implement his ambitious programs, he somehow had to bolster the republic's finances.

Lamar's idea involved improving trade relations between Texas and prosperous Santa Fe. Most Texans considered Santa Fe part of their country anyway, since the republic's western border extended three hundred miles straight north from the headwaters of the Rio Grande. If merchants could ship Cuban goods from the Gulf Coast directly across Texas to Santa Fe, rather than north to Missouri and then southwest via the Santa Fe Trail, they could shave hundreds of miles off their freight route. Lamar figured that the republic's coffers would fill rapidly if Texans took over the freighting for this rich and profitable trade.

In 1839, Lamar urged his congress to approve an expedition to Santa Fe to explore—and, he hoped—to confirm his trade theory. But nothing happened until April 1841, when Lamar sponsored the following announcement in the Austin *City Gazette:*

> *Having been authorized . . . to organize a military force for the purpose of opening a commercial inter-course with the people of Santa Fe; for which purpose troops are necessary to escort the merchandise through the Comanche wilderness. I therefore respectfully address myself to the young men of the country. . . . All who arm, mount and equip themselves will receive the pay of mounted gunmen. . . . Ten large road-wagons will be furnished by the government to the merchants. . . . [T]his expedition will furnish an ample field for adventure. . . .*

On June 20, 1841, between three hundred and four hundred men and boys, along with as many horses and a score of supply wagons, left Austin for Santa Fe. Before the trip was over, the Texan-Santa Fe Expedition would travel north to the Chihuahua Trail and then west across the parched Llano Estacado, to San Miguel, New Mexico.

One of the men who left Austin that day was George Wilkins Kendall, founder of the New Orleans *Picayune,* one of the most influ-ential newspapers in the South. He had decided to make "a tour of some kind upon the great Western Prairies, induced by the hope of correcting a derangement of health." In 1844, he would publish a his-tory of the expedition, which he claimed to have joined with the understanding that it was "commercial in its intentions." However, he soon learned that there were other reasons for the mission. He wrote:

> *General Lamar had an ulterior intention—that of bringing so much of the province of New Mexico as lies upon the eastern or Texan side of the Rio Grande under the protection of his government—I did not know until I was upon the march to Santa Fe. He was led to conceive this project by a well-founded belief that nine-tenths of the inhabitants were discontented under the Mexican yoke, and anxious to come under the protection of that flag to which they really owed fealty. . . . On its arrival at the destined point, should the inhabitants really manifest a disposition to declare their full allegiance to Texas, the flag of the single-star Republic would have been raised on the Government House at Santa Fe; but if not, the Texan commissioners were merely to make such arrangements with the authorities as would best tend to the opening of a trade, and then retire.*

As it turned out, the Mexican government considered the Texan-Santa Fe Expedition to be an invasion. It instructed New Mexico Governor Manuel Armijo to respond accordingly. He dispatched troops to arrest the Texans as soon as they crossed into his territory. And so, in the early fall of 1841, the Texans found themselves marching toward their original destination as military prisoners.

In October, the captives began a long and arduous march from San Miguel to Mexico City, where they were promptly thrown into jail. In April 1842, after tempers had waned, they were released and sent home.

THE PIG WAR

- 1841 -

To most of the residents of the small town of Austin, he was a genuine dandy, this thirty-year-old count from France. They could not understand why he insisted on being addressed by his full name, a real tongue twister: Jean Peter Isadore Alphonse Dubois, Comte de Saligny!

De Saligny was in Austin on official business, representing France as the charge d'affaires to the Republic of Texas. The highest-ranking French official in the country, he came from a background of wealth and luxurious living that had not prepared him for the wilds of Texas. So he tried to make up for what he perceived to be a lack of "civilized" comforts by building an expensive house complete with a wine cellar. He even imported a French chef.

The count had been living in Austin for about two years when he became a prime player in an incident that would thereafter be remembered as "the Pig War." It came to a head when de Saligny wrote a letter to Texas Secretary of State J. S. Mayfield and accused a man by the name of Bullock, manager of a local hotel, of callously attacking one of his servants, Eugene Pluyette. He called this act of supposedly unprovoked hostility "one of the most scandalous and outrageous violations of the Laws of Nations."

Mayfield had just begun to consider the charge when he received a letter from Bullock, who claimed that de Saligny and his servant had killed his hogs "maliciously and wantonly . . . with pitchforks and pistols"—a loss for which he said they owed him $275.75. What was a poor hotel owner to do? he asked. The law would not permit him to prosecute de Saligny because he had diplomatic immunity.

The matter escalated when Bullock threatened Pluyette again, and Mayfield called a hearing to attempt to sort out the details of the bizarre case. De Saligny was insulted that his case was to be considered by such a lowly Texas court. He suggested that it should be referred to an international court instead. He refused to attend Mayfield's hearing and ordered his servant, Pluyette, not to attend as well. Despite their absence, Bullock was bound over for trial.

At the trial, de Saligny explained why he and his servant had indeed killed Bullock's pigs:

> For a long time I have been tormented, and still am tormented every day, like everybody, from the numerous pigs that infest the city. Every morning one of my servants spends two hours repairing the boards of my fence that these animals break in order to eat my horse's corn; 140 pounds of nails have been used in this way!
>
> One day three pigs came even into my bedroom; ate the linen there and destroyed my papers. Another time a dozen of these animals, in order to eat the corn, rushed my stable and trampled one of my servants who

was rescued half dead. It was then that following all
my neighbors' example, I ordered my people to kill all
the pigs that should come into my yard. Did they
belong to Mr. Bullock or someone else? I do not know.

De Saligny said he tried to pay Bullock what he considered a fair price for the animals—$123.75—but the stubborn Texan had refused the money.

The final skirmish in the Pig War occurred a short time later, when Bullock assaulted the count. De Saligny demanded that Mayfield take immediate action, but the secretary simply responded that the case was under advisement. Dissatisfied with this answer, de Saligny pressed the issue, and Mayfield, who by now was growing weary of the entire affair, replied curtly that he would be happy to provide de Saligny with his passport.

The count left Texas immediately and, when he lodged a complaint with the French Foreign Ministry, France severed relations with the upstart republic. Unfortunately, a $5 million bond issue that Texas was negotiating with France at the time fell through as a result of de Saligny's outrage.

THE BROWNSVILLE
SECESSION CAMPAIGN

- 1850 -

TEXAS HAS HAD A STORMY POLITICAL LIFE. Once ruled by Spain and then by Mexico, it won its independence in 1836, when General Sam Houston defeated General Santa Anna at San Jacinto, near today's city of Houston. For a decade Texas existed as an independent republic, but many residents longed for the day when it would join the United States. That wish was granted in December 1845, sparking a war between the United States and its southern neighbor.

Political intrigue did not end with Texas statehood. Some residents wanted to return to the days of the republic. One of these was Joseph R. Palmer, editor of the Brownsville, Texas, newspaper, the *American Flag.* By early February 1850, he and some of his neighbors had decided they had suffered long enough from the ineptitude and indifference of politicians in Austin, and they intended to do something about it. Palmer flooded the region with handbills that read in part:

Fellow Citizens—The undersigned invite you to join
them in a public meeting, to be held in the town of
Brownsville, at the schoolhouse of Mr. R. N. Stansbury,
on Saturday, the 2nd of February, 1850, at 7 o'clock,
P.M., to take steps as are necessary for the organization
of the Rio Grande Territory!

The time has at length arrived, when the people of
this Valley must act with promptitude and decision. We
have too long confided in the justice of the people of
Texas—too long tamely submitted to her unauthorized
political jurisdiction. Our confidence in Texas has been
misplaced, and it behooves us to appeal to the Federal
Government for a territorial organization. We are enti-
tled to it. Let us knock at the door of Congress for that
protection which Texas denies us.

Many of the men who gathered at Stansbury's schoolhouse that
evening still had vivid memories of the recent war with Mexico over
the issue of Texas statehood. Many residents of the strip of land that
lay between the Rio Grande and the Nueces River held little allegiance to Texas, and the question of who had jurisdiction over that
large piece of real estate had never been decided with certainty.

At the end of the war, the town of Brownsville had grown up
almost overnight from a few shacks in a cotton field to a sizable community that boasted a wharf, warehouses, and merchants eager to do
business not only with nearby Mexico but with other states as well.
In the two years since the end of the war, native Mexicans and immigrant Americans had filed claims and counterclaims for the fertile
land that lay between the two rivers.

The audience in the smoke-filled schoolhouse listened intently as one landowner after another rose to speak his piece. When the rhetoric ended, the delegates representing Cameron, Starr, Webb, and Nueces Counties put together a series of resolutions that took issue with the relationship between residents of the region and politicians in Austin. Among other points, the signers of the document recommended "a convention, composed of delegates from the different sections of said territory, to devise a provisional government, with suspended functions, until our claims can be urged before Congress by a delegate chosen by the people." The convention was to be held in Brownsville on March 16.

In the meantime, leaders of the separatist movement wasted no time in presenting their grievances to the U.S. Congress. On February 27, New York senator William H. Seward introduced into the Senate a petition for a territorial government. Henry Clay of Kentucky presented another two weeks later. The proclamation read by Seward said in part:

> *THIS MEMORIAL of the citizens and residents of the Territory and Valley of the Rio Grande, respectfully represents that it is the desire of your memorialists that all that section of country East of the Rio Grande and South of the line of New Mexico, distinct from the former province of Texas, be erected into a territorial government, and that it be called the Territory of the Rio Grande.*

The petition was signed by 106 citizens, all but three of them of Mexican heritage. This led analysts of the situation to surmise that leaders of the movement had enticed "cross-mark patriots," so called because they were illiterate and signed their names with an "X," to endorse the document whether they understood its implications or not.

"What [the separatists'] object is I do not know," said Texas senator Thomas J. Rusk. "They have taken charge of the Mexican population, and are engaged in directing their action to their own purposes."

The first petition made little impact on the Senate. Several days later, when a baffled Clay presented a second version, he admitted, "I know very little on the subject. Indeed, when I received the letter accompanying the petition from a person with whom I am not at all acquainted, I had no information whatsoever that there was any dissatisfaction prevailing in that portion of the Country."

The second petition was signed by seventy-four leading settlers of the region in question, most of them white. But Congress still was unimpressed. Nothing became of the two petitions submitted by the Brownsville separatists.

Meanwhile, back in Texas, other settlers of the disputed land launched their own petition drive. Their document declared:

> [W]e fully recognize and assert the right of the State of Texas to the sovereignty and jurisdiction over the territory between the Nueces and the Rio Grande, and hold ourselves bound as citizens of the State, to sustain that right against internal opponents or external enemies.

When a tribunal was established to investigate the "legal and just titles to land situated between the Nueces and the Rio Grande," and to secure "to every citizen his just claims and homestead," the death knell was sounded for the Brownsville secession attempt. Within months, the issue was history, and Texas officials exercised their right to govern all of the newly established state.

THE BIRTH OF KING RANCH

- 1853 -

Steamboat captain Richard King could not have known in April 1852 that he was about to embark on one of the most profitable undertakings of his life. Sitting uncomfortably astride his big horse, the twenty-seven-year-old New Yorker scanned the endless Texas prairie. He was not accustomed to riding on horseback, and the 170-mile trip overland from Brownsville to Corpus Christi was tiring for a man more accustomed to traveling on water than on dry land.

King had successfully plied the murky waters of the Rio Grande for several years, carrying freight up and down the river. During the recent war with Mexico, he had supplied American troops with badly needed equipment—a job that had left him financially secure. Now he was in love with the seventeen-year-old daughter of the Presbyterian minister in Brownsville, and he had begun contemplating other business ventures that might help him to support a wife and family.

When King and a few companions reached Santa Gertrudis Creek, about forty-five miles southwest of Corpus Christi, they stopped to survey the landscape. It was good ground. Spanish explorer Alvar Núñez Cabeza de Vaca had journeyed through the same region more than three hundred years earlier and had remarked, "All over the land are vast and handsome pastures, with good grass for cattle; and it strikes me the soil would be very fertile were the country inhabited and improved by reasonable people."

More recently a local man named Thomas Dryer had described "thousands and tens of thousands of wild horses running in immense herds as far as the eye or telescope could sweep the horizon. The whole country seemed to be running!"

King was impressed with what he saw. In his mind's eye he was quick to convert the vast grassland into pasture for horses and cattle. Instinctively he decided on the course his future would take when he told his partner in the steamboat business:

> Land and livestock have a way of increasing in value.
> Cattle and horses, sheep and goats, will reproduce
> themselves into value. But boats—they have a way of
> wrecking, decaying, falling apart, decreasing in value
> and increasing in cost of operation.

After wrapping up some business in Corpus Christi, King met with an old friend, Texas Ranger Gideon "Legs" Lewis. The two men hammered out a partnership to establish a small ranch on the banks of a creek in South Texas. King was to provide the capital, while Lewis and his Ranger patrol would provide protection from Indians and rustlers. This proved to be the modest beginning of what one day would become the world's largest livestock operation, King Ranch.

Although busy with his ranch, King continued to run his steamboat business. As his cattle operation grew, he located the Mexican owners of the original Mexican land grant to which he had staked a claim and purchased 15,500 acres from them for $300. Shortly afterward, he added a Spanish land grant of 53,000 acres for which he paid $1,800. He built a house, barns, corrals, and a stockade. A visionary, he also dammed a small stream on the property. When a drought hit the area soon afterward, his was the only ranch with a good supply of water.

Over the next few years, the Santa Gertrudis ranch continued to grow. King and his foremen traveled across the Rio Grande to Mexico and bought cattle at ridiculously low prices. On one occasion, after buying all of the livestock in a particularly poor village, he offered to take part of the inhabitants back to the ranch and put them to work. This was the beginning of *Los Kineños,* the "King People," progenitors of generations of intensely loyal Mexican families who worked for King Ranch.

By the time the Civil War broke out in 1861, King was one of the largest landowners in Texas—if not the largest. With a wife and three children to care for, he had increased his holdings to many thousands of acres that supported twenty thousand head of cattle and three thousand horses. He had also initiated a series of livestock breeding experiments that he hoped would result in better, stronger, and longer-lived strains of horses and cattle. Combining the best characteristics of eastern breeds with the hardiness of Texas varieties, he eventually produced a new breed of cattle, the Santa Gertrudis, and a new type of mount, the quarter horse.

The Civil War devastated many Texas ranchers, but King saw a new opportunity to increase his holdings, improve his livestock, and support the Confederacy by providing transportation for the export of Texas cotton and the import of European firearms. After the war he continued to operate his large spread. He also invested heavily in a Corpus Christi newspaper, a railroad company, a stagecoach line, and an icehouse.

After King's death in 1885, his son-in-law, Robert Kleberg, took over the day-to-day operations of the ranch. Following in his mentor's footsteps, he and those family members who succeeded him turned King Ranch into the world's largest livestock operation, with branches in Pennsylvania, Kentucky, Cuba, Brazil, and Australia, among other properties. Truly, Richard King had lived up to his nickname, "the King of Texas."

A CARGO OF CAMELS

- 1856 -

RESIDENTS OF INDIANOLA, TEXAS, HAD LOOKED forward for almost two weeks to this day, May 14, 1856. They had heard rumors that a ship was floating just a few miles out in the Gulf of Mexico, waiting for the sea to calm so that she could dock at one of the long wharves that jutted into Matagorda Bay. Indianola was among the best seaports in the Lone Star State, and the town's citizens were used to seeing ships from all countries come and go. But today would be unique. Today the incoming ship carried a cargo few Texans had ever seen: camels!

All morning, curious spectators gathered at the docks and strained to spot the naval vessel on the far horizon. The news was that the *Supply*—the ship that had carried the animals across the Atlantic Ocean from the Middle East—was going to bring the camels into port.

Then the harbormaster received word that, because of bad weather in the gulf, the *Supply* had rendezvoused with another ship, the *Fashion,* off the coast of Louisiana and had transferred the camels to it. Finally, just before noon, the *Fashion* put into port at Indianola.

Almost the entire population of the town watched in amazement as the sailors aboard the *Fashion* dropped a gangplank and started leading the camels down the incline to the dock. According to Major Henry C. Wayne, the officer in charge of the strange cargo, the animals, once their feet hit dry ground, "became excited to an almost uncontrolled degree, rearing, kicking, crying out, breaking halters, tearing up pickets and by other fantastic tricks demonstrating their enjoyment of the 'Liberty of the soil.'"

The long trip over the Mediterranean, through the Strait of Gibraltar, and across the Atlantic Ocean had been relatively uneventful considering the fragile cargo the *Supply* had on board. Navy Lieutenant David D. Porter, who later gained fame in the Civil War as a Union admiral, had been responsible for acquiring the camels in the Middle East, and one of the first chores he performed upon returning home was to notify U.S. Secretary of War Jefferson Davis of his success. He wrote:

> *We have lost on the voyage but one of those we purchased . . . and she died from no want of care, but because she was not able to produce her young one. . . . We still have more than we started with, some young ones having been born on the passage, and are in fine condition. All the other camels I am happy to say have not received a scratch. . . . [T]hey are looking a little shabby just now, most of them shedding their hair . . . but they are fat and in good health.*

A year earlier, the U.S. Congress, at Davis's urging, had authorized "the importation of camels and dromedaries to be used for military purposes" and had earmarked thirty thousand dollars for the experiment. Davis, a veteran of the war with Mexico, had seen considerable service in the Desert Southwest. Keenly aware of the role that camels had played over the centuries in the warfare of other nations, he believed that the strange beasts could be put to good use in the United States as well.

After considerable planning, Major Wayne and Lieutenant Porter departed for North Africa, where they were met by a third American, Gwinn Harris Heap, whose father had been U.S. consul to Tunis for a number of years. After visiting several cities along the Mediterranean coast, the threesome acquired thirty-three camels before departing for home in February 1856.

Indianola was ready for the camels. Ten acres of land had been set aside for them, and a two-hundred-foot-long shed had been built to house them. Major Wayne decided first to acclimate the animals to the intense humidity of the Gulf Coast by letting them rest awhile in a large corral. Three weeks later, he assembled the animals for a 140-mile journey to San Antonio, the first leg of a trip that would eventually take them to El Paso, Albuquerque, and across the arid Southwest all the way to Fort Tejon, California.

To the amazement of all concerned, the camels performed extremely well. Capable of carrying loads of up to twelve hundred pounds—larger than a horse or mule could carry—the beasts of burden lumbered along at a slow but steady pace across the trackless desert. In an effort to establish a breeding program for the camels, Wayne, who had gone on to a desk job in Washington, D.C., wrote to Quartermaster General Thomas J. Jesup:

> *I have never entertained the idea, that the benefits to be derived from the introduction of the animal among us could be so extensively realized in our day. I regard*

it more in the light of a legacy to posterity of precisely
the same character as the introduction of the horse and
other domestic animals by the early settlers of America
have been to us.

But the great camel experiment eventually failed. With the advent of the Civil War, the personnel at Union garrisons in the Southwest scattered before the advancing Confederates. Matters more important than the formulation and maintenance of a camel corps soon occupied the minds of Union commanders. Some of the imported camels were set free and some were kept in captivity. The last known survivor died in a Los Angeles zoo in 1934, but even today people occasionally tell tales of seeing lone camels in remote corners of the Southwest.

SAM HOUSTON'S LAST HURRAH

- 1861 -

SAD AND ALONE, SAM HOUSTON LEANED BACK in his favorite wing chair in his bedroom at the governor's mansion in Austin. The sixty-eight-year-old leader sat for a spell, then got up and paced the floor for a few minutes and sat again. From time to time, he rubbed his sore thigh, a reminder of an arrow wound he had received when he fought beside his mentor, Andrew Jackson, in the Creek Wars of 1814.

Thirty-five years had passed since Houston had resigned from the governorship of Tennessee and migrated to Texas. Now, after serving as president of the short-lived Republic of Texas and as a U.S. senator from Texas, the towering giant of a man was governor of his adopted state, and he was saddled with a whole new set of problems. It was March 15, 1861, and the dilemma Houston faced was the overwhelming pro-secession mood that had gripped Texas since the end of January. Six other southern states had already left the Union and formed the Confederate States of America. On January 28, the Texas house of representatives had endorsed secession by a vote of

166 to 8. On February 23, in a popular referendum, Texans had voted 46,129 to 14,697 in favor of secession.

Known to have expressed antisecession sentiments in the past, Houston was losing popularity with the people. Some voters even went so far as to call him a traitor. "I, a traitor to Texas?" the hero of San Jacinto would respond bitterly. "Was it for this I bared my bosom to the hail of battle—to be branded a traitor in my old age?"

But hurtful remarks were not enough to keep Houston from traveling across the state to urge his constituents not to make hasty, ill-considered decisions about secession. In Galveston on February 18, he implored a large crowd to reconsider the matter and unsuccessfully tried to reason with them. He pleaded:

> *Some of you laugh to scorn the idea of bloodshed as the result of secession. But let me tell you what is coming. Your fathers and husbands, your sons and brothers, will be herded at the point of a bayonet. You may, after the sacrifice of countless millions of treasure and hundreds of thousands of lives, as a bare possibility, win Southern independence . . . but I doubt it. I tell you that, while I believe with you in the doctrine of state rights, the North is determined to preserve this Union. They are not a fiery, impulsive people as you are, for they live in colder climates. But when they begin to move in a given direction, they move with the steady momentum and perseverance of a mighty avalanche; and what I fear is, they will overwhelm the South.*

On March 5, despite Governor Houston's impassioned pleas, the Secession Convention announced that Texas was breaking away from the United States and apprised citizens that it would apply for admission to the Confederacy. Officials of the convention instructed all existing state officers, including Houston, to swear an oath of allegiance to the Confederacy within the next ten days. When March 15 arrived and Houston had made no effort to make his pledge, a message was delivered to the governor's mansion advising him that he would be replaced as governor the following day if he did not comply with the demand by noon.

Years later, Houston's daughter, Nancy, fifteen years old at the time, wrote of the impasse:

> *After bidding his family good night the General left positive instructions with Mrs. Houston that he must not be disturbed under any circumstances and that no visitors were to be admitted to the mansion. He then went to his bedroom on the upper floor, removed his coat and vest and shoes and remained alone throughout the night, during which he did not sleep. Instead he walked the floor of his bedroom and the upper hall in his sock feet, wrestling with his spirit as Jacob wrestled with the angel until the purple dawn of another day shone over the eastern hills. He had come through his Gethsemane, and the die was cast. When he came down and met Mrs. Houston, he said "Margaret, I will never do it."*

The next day, Houston reported to the capitol building in Austin. Years later an eyewitness described the events that followed:

> As I look back into the darkness of those days, the central figure of them all is that of the old governor sitting in his chair in the basement of the capitol, sorrowfully meditating what it were best to do. The officer of the gathering upstairs summoned the old man three times to come forward and take the oath of allegiance to the Confederacy. I remember as yesterday the call thrice repeated—"Sam Houston! Sam Houston! Sam Houston!" but the man sat silent, immovable, in his chair.

Minutes after Houston refused to take the oath, his lieutenant governor, Edward Clark, replaced him as governor of Texas. Two and a half years later, Houston uttered his last words, "Texas . . . Texas," and died.

THE BATTLE AT SABINE PASS

- 1863 -

FOR SEVERAL WEEKS NOW, Lieutenant Richard W. Dowling and his command of Confederate Texan Davis Guards had gazed ruefully over the ramparts of Fort Griffin. General John Bankhead Magruder had ordered Dowling and his men to occupy this site near the mouth of the Sabine River and guard against a Union invasion from New Orleans. But as August 1863 came to a close, and as day after day passed uneventfully, the forty-four soldiers began to think that they would sit through the entire Civil War without ever firing a shot at the enemy.

Dowling was an Irishman and a former saloon owner in Houston. Most of his command were Irish dockworkers and stevedores from the Houston area, "men of brawn and muscle," as they were once characterized; "quiet in manner if you treated them right, but woe to you if you offended one." They had seen limited action so far during the war. However, Dowling, described as "a modest, retiring, boyish-looking Irish lad," had helped recapture Galveston from a

Union blockade in January 1863, before being assigned command of the small earthen stockade called Fort Griffin.

Sometimes during the lazy summer afternoons, Dowling and his men would entertain themselves by firing at range markers floating in the middle of the Sabine River. There was nothing else to do, and Dowling rationalized that someday the gunnery practice might come in handy. By September, the cannoneers had become proficient with the few artillery pieces that made up the fort's batteries, and each man had a keen sense of the distance from the ramparts to various points on the river.

In early September 1863, Union General Nathaniel P. Banks, in a prelude to the massive Red River campaign that he would launch the following March, sent a flotilla of boats toward the mouth of the Sabine River. In the fleet were the gunboats *Clifton, Sachem, Granite City,* and *Arizona,* as well as twenty-two transportation crafts. These were accompanied by five thousand Union soldiers. All that lay between the large, well-armed command and Texas was tiny Fort Griffin, the Texan Davis Guards, and about 150 infantrymen under the command of Captain F. H. Odlum.

To Union strategists, the job of leveling the Confederate fort looked simple. While the gunboats fired on the ramparts, a landing party of five hundred soldiers would work its way behind the structure and attack the unprotected rear. With Fort Griffin disabled, it would be a simple task to proceed down the Texas coast toward the cities of Galveston, Beaumont, and Houston. On September 8, already tasting victory, Banks ordered his fleet into the mouth of the Sabine.

As the morning passed, Dowling and his artillerists watched the four Union gunboats steam slowly up the Sabine. When they drew within range, the *Clifton* opened fire and dropped twenty-six rounds into the deadly silent fort. The craft dropped back downriver to report that it had received no opposing fire.

Around four o'clock, the *Clifton,* this time accompanied by the *Sachem,* again approached the fort. Closer and closer the two crafts came, until they were well within range of Dowling's artillery. The jaunty Irishman gave the command to fire, and his expert gunners, calling on the experience they had gained from their practice firing at the range markers, let go with everything they had.

They needed only four shots to hit the Sachem. As it drifted like a sitting duck in the shallow river, its commander ordered his men to raise the white flag. Thirty minutes later, after running aground near the fort, the paralyzed *Clifton* likewise surrendered. More than four hundred Union troops were captured during the melee. The remaining two gunboats and all of the transports fled from the mouth of the Sabine and steamed for New Orleans.

The failure of the Union to destroy Fort Griffin delayed its invasion of Texas by at least a month. Lieutenant Dowling and his Davis Guards became heroes overnight. Local residents were so grateful that they insisted that officials reward the men's bravery. Medals made from shaved silver dollars and hung from green ribbons were presented to Dowling and all of his command. On one side of each medal was a likeness of the Maltese cross, while the other side displayed the words, "Battle of Sabine Pass, September 8, 1863."

Calling the battle "the Thermopylae of the Civil War," Confederate President Jefferson Davis awarded all of Dowling's command the Davis Guard Medal. It was the only medal the Confederacy ever awarded for valor.

THE EMANCIPATION OF JUNETEENTH

- 1865 -

AFRICAN AMERICANS IN TEXAS STILL JOYOUSLY REMEMBER events of June 19, 1865. It was on that date—two months after the main Confederate armies surrendered to the Union—that Major General Gordon Granger stepped off a ship at Galveston and, on behalf of the new president, Andrew Johnson, issued a historic declaration: "The people of Texas are informed that, in accordance with a proclamation from the Executive of the United States, all slaves are free."

Of course, President Lincoln had issued his Emancipation Proclamation more than two years earlier, on January 1, 1863. But Texas slaveholders had ignored it, and most Texas slaves, kept ignorant by their masters, never even knew of its existence. By war's end, about a quarter of a million slaves still toiled in the homes, factories, and fields of the Lone Star State.

On the eve of the Civil War, Texas had a slave population of about 186,000. Black men, women, and children were vital to the state's economy, as they produced almost all of the marketable crops. Others put in long days spinning thread and making cloth. They worked for their entire lives under sometimes cruel conditions without hope of pay or freedom. Nonetheless, when a special committee of the state legislature looked into their conditions, it came to the dubious conclusion that they were "the happiest . . . human beings on whom the sun shines." Decades later one slave woman would contradict that assessment with her recollection that "slavery time was hell."

When the Civil War began, 90 percent of all Texans could claim a southern heritage. So it was no surprise when, in 1861, they voted by a three-to-one margin to secede from the Union and join the Confederacy. The state constitution was amended to prohibit emancipation.

As the federal armies advanced, Texas became a refuge for many Southerners, including thousands of panicky slaveholders who brought their slaves with them. By the time Granger stepped onto the wharf at Galveston, the slave population in Texas had increased by 35 percent.

June 19—or Juneteenth, as it came to be known—marked the true death of black Texans' back-breaking bondage. It was a day of jubilee. One euphoric slave, Molly Harrell, recalled that "we all walked down the road singing and shouting to beat the band." Another woman tossed her child into the air shrieking, "Tamar, you'se free!" Yet another announced with satisfaction, "Mrs. Dellie kain't whoope me no mo're."

But freedom was only the first step in a long and perilous process. Suddenly, former slaves had to find a source of income. Many wanted to search for relatives who had been sold to other masters. Most were eager to leave the scenes of their enslavement, often setting out with nothing more than a bundle they could carry on their backs. A few remained behind in loyalty to their former owners.

Today more than two million African Americans make their homes in Texas. They and others who value freedom continue to celebrate the emancipation of Texas slaves on Juneteenth.

THE SALT CREEK PRAIRIE MASSACRE

- 1871 -

GENERAL WILLIAM TECUMSEH SHERMAN LISTENED in disbelief as Thomas Brazeal, an army teamster, told his story. Sherman had just arrived at Fort Richardson the previous day, May 16, 1871, on an inspection tour of Texas. For months he had received complaints from terrified Texans that relations with the Indians, especially along the northern border with Indian Territory, were growing more and more hostile. But federal authorities thought the Texans were making up stories of Indian raids simply to draw Reconstruction troops out of central Texas, so they took them with a grain of salt. Sherman had finally decided to see for himself whether conditions on the frontier were as bad as he had been told.

Now, at the post hospital, Brazeal was telling Sherman about a bloody massacre that had taken place earlier in the day. The teamster was one of five people who had escaped an attack by Kiowa Indians on a wagon train carrying government supplies to Fort Richardson from nearby Fort Griffin. The wagon master and six other teamsters

had been killed during the brief encounter at a place called Salt Creek
Prairie, some twenty-two miles west of Fort Richardson. Sherman,
who had been responsible during the Civil War for a fifty-mile-wide
path of death and destruction from Atlanta to Savannah, flinched as
he heard that one of the teamsters, Sam Elliott, had been roasted—
most likely while he was still alive.

But it wasn't the massacre and the theft by the Kiowas of forty-
one mules that alarmed Sherman the most. What really disturbed
him was the fact that he and his small entourage had crossed the same
prairie the day before. He knew that he very well could have been a
massacre victim himself. Indeed, what Sherman didn't know until
some time later was that an old Kiowa medicine man, Mamanti, had
stopped an attack on Sherman's wagons when he had a vision that a
larger and more rewarding train would soon be coming by. The
Kiowas, under the leadership of chiefs Satank, Satanta, and Big Tree,
deferred to the medicine man's prophecy and waited for the supply
train. As a result, General Sherman's life was spared.

After hearing Brazeal's horrible story, the post surgeon and a
small detail of men rode to Salt Creek Prairie to gather up the bodies of the dead teamsters. The tough soldiers were aghast at what they
found. The surgeon later wrote:

> *All the bodies were riddled with bullets, covered with
> gashes, and the skulls crushed, evidently with an ax
> found bloody on the place; some of the bodies also
> exhibited signs of having been stabbed with arrows.*
>
> *One of the bodies was even more mutilated than
> the others, it having been found fastened with a chain
> to a pole of a wagon lying over a fire with the face to
> the ground, the tongue being cut out. Because of the*

charred condition of the soft parts, it was impossible to
determine whether the man was burned before or after
his death.

Sherman accompanied an armed detail to Fort Sill, Indian Territory, to find the culprits. At the fort, the Indian agent questioned the
Kiowa chiefs about the massacre, and Satanta quietly but boldly
admitted that he was responsible for the attack. "If any other Indian
claims the honor of leading that party he will be lying to you. I led it
myself," declared the proud warrior.

Satanta, Satank, and Big Tree were arrested and taken to Jacks-
boro, the civilian community outside the gates of Fort Richardson.
Satank, the oldest of the three, had no intention of being tried in a
white man's court. Shortly after leaving Fort Sill, he worked his wrists
and ankles free from his manacles and jumped from a wagon. A
guard shot and killed him.

A civilian court quickly found Satanta and Big Tree guilty of murder and sentenced them to hang. However, under pressure from federal officials advocating the "peace policy" of President Ulysses Grant,
the court reduced the sentences to life imprisonment. Later, Texas
Governor Edmund J. Davis pardoned the pair. Although Sherman
was a close friend and supporter of President Grant, he was furious
about the two men's release from prison. In a letter to Davis, he wrote:

I believe in making a tour of your frontier, with a
small escort, I ran the risk of my life, and I said to the
military commander what I now say to you, that I will
not again voluntarily assume that risk in the interest of
your frontier, that I believe Satanta and Big Tree will
have their revenge, if they have not already had it, and

that if they are to have scalps, that yours is the first
that should be taken.

Fears that Satanta and Big Tree would continue to commit crimes against whites proved valid. By 1878, Satanta was back in prison in Huntsville. He simply could not adapt to the white man's ways. He once declared, "I don't want to settle. I love to roam over the prairie. . . . These soldiers cut down my timber, they kill my buffalo, and when I see that, it feels as if my heart would burst with sorrow."

Rather than serve his sentence, Satanta leaped from the prison hospital window and killed himself. Big Tree was also arrested again, but again he was released. After this final brush with the law, he lived quietly and died in Oklahoma in 1929.

BILLY DIXON'S REMARKABLE SHOT

~ 1874 ~

IF THERE WAS ONE FACET OF BILLY DIXON'S LIFE of which he was most
proud, it was his career as a buffalo hunter, or more specifically a hide
hunter. Although he was only twenty-three years old, he had already
won the admiration and respect of hunters many years his senior. He
was known all over Texas, Kansas, and Indian Territory for his marksmanship and his ability to bring down staggering numbers of buffalo
in the course of a single day.

But on June 29, 1874, Dixon wasn't thinking about buffalo. The
young hunter was concerned about his safety and that of his twenty-
five or so companions. For the past three days, they had been holed up
at a remote hunters' camp in the Texas Panhandle called Adobe Walls,
fighting off a brutal attack by Comanche, Kiowa, and Cheyenne warriors under the leadership of Isa-tai and Quanah Parker. Three men
had already died in the fierce fighting, which pitted the handful of
hunters against nearly seven hundred Indians. The warriors had also
shot and killed most of the hunters' horses and cattle. Had it not been

for the thick walls of sod, more casualties would likely have occurred inside Adobe Walls.

For two days after the initial attack, it had been fairly quiet in the hunters' compound. One man slipped away to Dodge City for help, while a burial detail interred the three dead men in a single grave. The hunters also disposed of the rotting carcasses of the cattle and horses as best they could. The Indians still surrounded Adobe Walls at a distance, showing themselves from time to time to remind the men inside that escape was impossible.

While several of the hunters surveyed the plain around the camp, they noticed some Indians silhouetted against a slight rise about a mile away. One of the hunters was Dixon, who had lost his prize Sharps rifle several days earlier while crossing the swollen Canadian River. Now, he reached over and picked up James Hanrahan's .50-caliber Sharps and fiddled for a moment with the rear sights. He aimed the rifle at a lone Indian outlined against the skyline. The big Sharps belched flames and smoke. Neither Dixon, his friends, nor the Indian's companions could believe their eyes. Dixon later described the incident:

> I took careful aim and pulled the trigger. We saw an Indian fall from his horse. The others dashed out of sight and behind a clump of timber. A few moments later two Indians ran quickly on foot to where the dead Indian lay, seized his body and scurried for cover. They had risked their lives, as we had frequently observed, to rescue a companion who might be not only wounded, but dead. I was admittedly a good marksman, yet this was what might be called a scratch shot.

Dixon's fluke shot was too much for the Indians. They left Adobe Walls to the buffalo hunters. Once they were out of sight, a curious hunter paced off the distance of Dixon's remarkable shot and found that it was 1,538 yards—nearly seven-eighths of a mile!

Out of the dramatic battle at Adobe Walls, two legends were born. One concerned the marksmanship of Billy Dixon. Although he repeatedly acknowledged that he had been lucky, his marksmanship became a subject for storytellers forever after.

Dixon went on to become a distinguished scout for the Sixth U.S. Cavalry under the command of Colonel Nelson Miles. He was awarded a Medal of Honor in 1874 for his "skill, courage and determined fortitude, displayed in an engagement with 5 others, on the 12th of September, 1874, against hostile Indians in overwhelming numbers." The U.S. Army later rescinded the award after learning that Dixon had been a civilian at the time.

The other legend spawned by Adobe Walls was the accuracy and killing power of the Sharps rifle. The Sharps had already been used by both North and South during the Civil War, but it was the hide hunters who made it so popular. It was the weapon of choice for hundreds of buffalo hunters who scoured the Great Plains in search of ever-dwindling herds during the 1870s and 1880s. To these men, the beauty of the Sharps was its ability to fire a heavy bullet several hundred yards with complete accuracy. Since the hunters usually shot their prey from a distance of at least three hundred yards, to keep from spooking other members of the herd, the long-range Sharps was ideal. Its reputation continued to grow as tales of Dixon's mile-long shot spread.

By the 1880s, buffalo had all but disappeared from the southern Great Plains. One reason for the mass extinction was hide hunters such as Dixon wielding sure-fire weapons such as the Sharps rifle. But another factor entered into the equation. The U.S.

government condoned the slaughter of the once-numerous bison as a means of controlling and "civilizing" the various Plains Indian tribes who depended upon the animal for their livelihood.

In 1875, when Texas legislators were considering a bill to protect the last of the state's buffalo herds, General Philip Sheridan appeared before the lawmakers and urged them to kill the proposal. In Sheridan's opinion, the men who destroyed the buffalo were heroes. They should be given "a hearty, unanimous vote of thanks," he said, as well as a bronze medal "with a dead buffalo on one side and a discouraged Indian on the other." Sheridan continued:

> *These men have done in the last two years, and will do in the next year, more to settle the vexed Indian question than the entire regular army has done in the last twenty years. They are destroying the Indians' commissary; and it is a well-known fact that an army losing its base of supplies is placed at a great disadvantage. Send them the powder and lead, if you will; but for the sake of a lasting peace, let them kill, skin and sell until the buffaloes are exterminated. Then your prairies can be covered with speckled cattle and the festive cowboy, who follows the hunter as a second forerunner of an advanced civilization.*

WAITING FOR THE "SUNSET"

- 1877 -

EARLY ON THE EVENING OF FEBRUARY 19, 1877, some eight thousand residents of the San Antonio area gathered by torchlight and paraded through town. Local officials had arranged the festivities to help celebrate the arrival of the Sunset, the first train ever to reach San Antonio. Twenty-five years in the planning, the rail line—part of the Galveston, Harrisburg, and San Antonio Railway—was welcomed gratefully by the local residents, whose community, one of the scheduled speakers said, was "perhaps the largest city on the continent . . . that had remained so long without railroad connection."

The parade was grander than any seen by the townspeople before. Thousands of participants marched up one street and down another, led by men carrying four tall standards festooned with American flags and Chinese lanterns. Also among the marchers were the Tenth U.S. Infantry band, representatives of the U.S. Cavalry, the Alamo Rifles, and a plethora of state and local government officials, including Governor Richard B. Hubbard, Lieutenant Governor Wells Thompson, and the mayors of Austin, Galveston, and San Antonio.

The newspapers had a field day with the evening's events. On February 19, the *San Antonio Express* reported that "San Antonio can now take a position in the great family of first class-cities and move grandly on to that greatness and prosperity that could never have been reached without the aid of the iron horse." The next day, the newspaper proclaimed in its headlines:

> *The Grand Celebration*
> *San Antonio in a Halo of Glory*
> *She Celebrates a Victory Over Time*
> *And Honors Her Guests Right Royally*
> *The Pomp and Grandeur of Parade*
> *Shining Light and Colors Bright*
> *8,000 People Put Forth Their Hands*
> *To Welcome Our Invited Guests*

The festivities of the evening were not confined to the marchers in the parade. The management of the Menger Hotel on Alamo Plaza decked the building with an unforgettable array of lights and Chinese lanterns. An awestruck eyewitness reported that the entire affair was a

> *scene of dazzling splendor that is seldom witnessed by*
> *any people, and almost beggared description. The lib-*
> *eral and patriotic proprietors of the Menger had dressed*
> *their immense establishment in glittering attire that*
> *shed bright light upon the entire plaza, and even the*
> *dark and frowning old Alamo brightened up, and*
> *seemed to come out of the gloom of its ancient tragedies*
> *and partake of the cheerful influences of its surround-*
> *ings. Pendants on ropes running from the top of the*

flagstaff on the Menger to the front cornice of the
building, were thickly hung with two rows of Chinese
lanterns forming a triangle of . . . lights, and a row of
the same kind of lanterns hung from the door of the
balcony.

The arrival of the railroad in San Antonio had an immediate impact upon the growth of the city and the welfare of its residents. A perceptive reporter for the *Texas Sun* of Houston was quick to recognize the value of train service. He wrote:

It does not require the ken of a prophet to predict some-
thing of the future of this old city, but so recently
touched by the magic wand of modern progress. . . .
Besides from this point stretches out a region known as
Western Texas, which contains . . . untold and unde-
veloped resources.

Within weeks, a depot was completed, as well as "hundreds of airy structures which have sprung up like mushrooms in a night, about it," the newspaper said. From November 1877 through January 1878, more than two thousand tourists registered at the Menger Hotel alone. The city's other hotels and boarding houses were equally crowded with visitors from as far away as New York City, Chicago, Baltimore, Kansas City, Boston, Detroit, and Cincinnati. By 1880 the population of Bexar County had grown to nearly thirty-one thousand residents, an increase of almost 100 percent in a decade. Many of the newcomers no doubt came at least in part because of the railroad.

Another impact of the railroad on Bexar County was a dramatic increase in agricultural production. The number of farms in the region quadrupled during the 1870s. As the rails linked the region with potential new markets, annual wool production rose from about seven hundred thousand pounds in 1872 to almost seven million pounds in 1884.

For years, residents of Bexar County had waited for the railroad to bring them the amenities of the East. Now that the rails had reached them, people were quick to grasp the potential of this new mode of transportation and to make it a part of their everyday lives. The modern age had arrived at last!

THE TIME THE TEXAS RANGERS LOST

- 1877 -

Solomon Schutz tried to remain calm as he blurted his message to the telegraph operator in Franklin, Texas (today's city of El Paso). The clerk nervously scribbled the words on paper and handed them to Schutz to double-check. The telegram was addressed to Colonel Edward Hatch, the U.S. Army commandant at Fort Bayard, located a little more than one hundred miles to the west in New Mexico. The message read:

> *Don Louis Cardis was killed this moment by Charles Howard, and we are expecting a terrible catastrophe in the county, as threats have been made that every American would be killed if harm came to Cardis. Can you not send us immediate help, for God's sake?*

Schutz shoved the paper back to the clerk, nodded his head in approval, and walked back down the street to his store, where the murder had occurred just minutes earlier. It was Wednesday afternoon, October 10, 1877. When Schutz reached the store, his brother, Joseph, was talking to the undertaker who had come to retrieve Cardis's body. Joseph was explaining how Judge Charles Howard had walked calmly in the front door of the store with a double-barreled shotgun and emptied one barrel into his victim's legs and the other into his chest. Then Howard had left the store and walked across the street to the Custom House, where his friend Joe Magoffin, the customs inspector, had advised him to get out of town. Rumors were already circulating that Howard had left quietly for Mesilla, New Mexico, a short distance up the Rio Grande.

The Howard-Cardis fracas had begun over a seemingly innocuous commodity: salt. Howard, a Missouri lawyer and a Democrat, had only recently arrived in the area, and he had immediately rubbed the overwhelmingly Republican citizenry the wrong way. When he attempted to stake a claim to some nearby salt lakes from which the local Mexican Americans had freely gathered salt for centuries, he alienated some powerful forces. Ultimately, he had threatened to kill Cardis, a one-time political ally who had recently written in his diary, "Captain Courtney advised me to be on the lookout, for Howard is making desperate threats at my life."

When Howard walked away from the crime a free man, the local Mexican Americans furiously plotted their revenge. They were already angry because Howard had signed a bond to leave El Paso County, never to return. Now, in the eyes of the local population, he was guilty of two crimes: murder and violating his bond.

The town of Franklin was so far removed from other communities in the state that a plea for Texas Rangers to help keep the peace went unheeded. So Major John B. Jones of the Frontier Battalion decided to form a temporary unit of rangers to be commanded by John B. Tays, a local man with no previous law-enforcement experience. In the meantime, when a group of Mexican-American farmers visited the nearby lakes to gather salt, Howard, still a free man, decided to prosecute them for trespassing on his property. On Wednesday, December 12, with warrants in hand, he rode to San Elizario, a few miles down the Rio Grande from Franklin, and there he caught up with the newly formed ranger detachment at its recently established headquarters. After eating supper with the rangers, Howard walked down the street to the Ellis Store, which was quickly surrounded by disgruntled Mexican Americans.

For the next five days, the mob laid siege to the Ellis Store and the rangers' headquarters down the street. Finally, on the morning of December 17, Howard decided to surrender in order to save the rest of his compatriots.

Later in the day the temporary ranger detachment was persuaded to surrender as well with the promise that they could keep their weapons and that they would be released unharmed. Within minutes, the Mexican Americans took the entire group into custody with the intention of executing Howard and two of the others.

The mob shot Howard first. As he lay dying in the dust, one of the Mexican-American men struck at him with his machete. Howard rolled out of the way just in time, and the angry man cut off two of his own toes. The rest of the mob finished off the judge.

One of the other victims, John Atkinson, fared little better. He begged his executioners to let him die with honor, then bared his chest and said, "When I give the word, fire at my heart—Fire!" Five shots entered his stomach, and he pleaded, "Higher up!" Two more rounds found their mark, but it took a pistol shot to his head to complete the business. The third man was unceremoniously shot. After the executions, the mob looted the town.

By Christmas, local law-enforcement officers, a regular patrol of Texas Rangers, and a contingent of "Buffalo Soldiers" had descended on San Elizario and restored peace, more or less. The so-called "El Paso Salt War" was over. On December 28, Lieutenant Tays buried two of the executed men in a village graveyard and transported Howard's body back to Franklin for interment. A congressional board of inquiry was called, and it recommended, among other things, the reestablishment of nearby Fort Bliss, which had been evacuated a year earlier.

For the Texas Rangers, the entire affair had been an embarrassment. The episode went down in the annals of Texas history as the only incident in which rangers voluntarily surrendered to an enemy.

THE VIOLENT DEATH OF
AN OUTLAW LEGEND

- 1878 -

FOR THE THIRD TIME IN AS MANY DAYS, Sam Bass, Seaborn Barnes, and Frank Jackson rode into the small town of Round Rock, Texas, to take a final look at its layout before robbing its only bank. A fourth member of the gang, Jim Murphy, had stayed behind in their camp at Old Round Rock. It was Friday, July 19, 1878, and no one appeared to pay much attention as the three horsemen rode up a back alley, hitched their mounts, and went into a store next door to the bank to buy some tobacco.

But from a distance, two men watched the threesome as they entered the store, made their purchases, and chatted with the clerk. They were Morris Moore, a former Texas Ranger who now served as a deputy sheriff for Travis County, and his partner, a man named Grimes, who was a deputy sheriff for Williamson County, which included the town of Round Rock. Texas Rangers had informed the pair that Bass and his men might attempt a bank robbery in the town. The rangers warned them not to try arresting the outlaws until the rangers showed up, but the two approached the store anyway.

Grimes entered and asked Barnes if he was armed. In an instant, Barnes drew his weapon and fired several times, killing Grimes instantly. Before Moore could react, he was shot through the chest and seriously wounded. The only casualty suffered by any of the Bass gang was a gunshot wound to Bass's finger.

The commotion roused three Texas Rangers—Dick Ware, George Harrell, and Chris Connor—who had been hiding in town waiting for the bank robbery attempt. They opened fire, and for several minutes, bullets flew wildly. Bass was wounded again, this time seriously, and Barnes was killed. Jackson somehow managed to pull Bass onto a horse behind him and ride to safety through the hail of gunfire.

Jackson and Bass galloped past their camp, where their cohort, Murphy, was waiting for them. Unknown to them, Murphy had betrayed his comrades by alerting the rangers to their presence. But he had understood that the rangers would make their move during the robbery, and since the robbery was not supposed to occur until the following day, Murphy was confused. He later remarked,

> *I was sitting in a door at Old Round Rock as they*
> *came by, and Frank was holding Bass on his horse. Bass*
> *looked pale and sickly, and his hand was bleeding, and*
> *he seemed to be working cartridges into his pistol. Jack-*
> *son looked at me as much as to say, "Jim, save yourself*
> *if you can. . . . I then saw Major Jones [of the Texas*
> *Rangers] go by, and hallooed to him, but he did not*
> *hear me. I then went into the new town; there was a*
> *good deal of excitement, and someone asked who the*
> *dead man was. I said . . . it must be Seaborn Barnes.*

Someone asked how they would know. I said he has got four bullet holes in his legs—three in his right and one in his left leg, which he got at Mesquite. They found the wounds, and was going to arrest me, when Major Jones came up, and shortly after recognized me, and I went down with him and identified the dead body as that of Seaborn Barnes.

The next day, rangers found Bass lying under a tree north of town. "Don't shoot," he exclaimed. "I am the man you are looking for. I am Sam Bass." The outlaw had been shot in the back, and his right kidney was damaged severely.

The rangers took the outlaw to Round Rock to interrogate him. Although they demanded that he name his confederates, Bass refused to the end. He died on July 21, 1878, his twenty-seventh birthday. He and his compatriot, Seaborn Barnes, are buried in a small cemetery in Round Rock.

Bass was a legend in his own time. Born in Indiana, he moved to Texas as a young man, took up a gun, and began robbing stagecoaches. This led to an even more profitable career as a train robber. In his book *The Texas Rangers, A Century of Frontier Defense,* Walter Prescott Webb claims that Bass and his men held up four trains within twenty miles of Dallas during a fifty-day period in 1878.

Webb described Bass as an outlaw whose "reputation as a bandit has never been surpassed." Although his criminal career lasted only about four years, the transplanted badman left an indelible mark on Texas folklore and history.

THE COURT-MARTIAL
OF HENRY FLIPPER

- 1881 -

ON DECEMBER 8, 1881, A CROWD OF CURIOUS ONLOOKERS gathered in front of the chapel at Fort Davis, Texas. After two months of deliberations, a verdict was about to be rendered in the court-martial of Lieutenant Henry Ossian Flipper, who had been charged with embezzlement after reporting that funds were missing from the post's commissary. However, in reality, Flipper, who was acting officer in charge of the commissary, was on trial more for his skin color than for dishonesty. The preponderance of evidence indicated that he was most likely framed.

Colonel Benjamin Henry Grierson, the white commander of the all-black Tenth Cavalry, had no doubt about Flipper's innocence. He wrote that the young officer

> *came under my immediate command . . . during the*
> *campaign against Victorio's band of hostile Indians,*

and from personal observations, I can testify to his effi-
ciency and gallantry in the field. . . . He has repeatedly
been selected for special and important duties, and dis-
charged them faithfully and in a highly satisfactory
manner.

Anxious spectators watched as Flipper, a six-foot, two-inch former slave from Georgia and the first black man ever to graduate from
the U.S. Military Academy at West Point, entered the building. His
accuser, the former commandant of Fort Davis, Colonel William R.
"Pecos Bill" Shafter, soon followed.

After the last of the testimony, Flipper's attorney, Major Merritt
Barber, summed up the true purpose of the trial in his closing argu-
ments. "The question before you is whether it is possible for a col-
ored man to secure and hold a position as an officer of the Army," he
said. Flipper and his lawyer would soon find out.

The senior officer ordered Flipper and Barber to stand while he
read the verdict of the court-martial panel. The twenty-five-year-old
lieutenant was found innocent of the embezzlement charge, but he
was found guilty of "conduct unbecoming an officer" and so was dis-
honorably discharged from the army. Despite criticism of the sentence by Robert Todd Lincoln, the U.S. secretary of war and
Abraham Lincoln's son, Flipper was cashiered out of the service to
which he had devoted so much of his life.

Flipper was devastated. Here was a man who had excelled in every
military mission he had ever undertaken. Liberian authorities had been
so impressed with his record at West Point that they tried to persuade
him to come to their country to lead their entire army. Instead, the
young lieutenant joined Troop A, Tenth U.S. Cavalry and so became
the only black officer of the all-black "Buffalo Soldiers."

The four regiments of Buffalo Soldiers—the Ninth and Tenth Cavalries along with the Twenty-fourth and Twenty-fifth Infantries—had been organized in 1866 to accommodate the vast number of recently freed slaves from the South who had entered military service during the last days of the Civil War. They were eventually sent west, and in the next few years, the outstanding regiments, all of them commanded by white officers, fought in many major battles with Indians. They were one of the most effective weapons in the army's arsenal during the Indian wars of the 1870s and 1880s.

Colonel Grierson expressed the prevailing attitude of career army officers toward the Buffalo Soldiers when he once remarked:

> *The officers and enlisted men have cheerfully endured*
> *many hardships and privations, and in the midst of*
> *great dangers steadfastly maintained a most gallant and*
> *zealous devotion to duty . . . and they may well be*
> *proud of the record made, and rest assured that the hard*
> *work undergone in the accomplishment of such . . .*
> *valuable service to their country cannot fail, sooner or*
> *later, to meet with due recognition and reward.*

In addition to their assignments in the West, the Buffalo Soldiers went on to fight in the Spanish-American War, where they helped other elements of the U.S. Army overrun Spanish defenses on the island of Cuba. They served in the Philippines, and in 1916 they rode into Mexico in pursuit of the bandit Pancho Villa, led by one of their old officers, General John J. "Black Jack" Pershing (the name "Black Jack" stemmed from Pershing's former duty with the Tenth Cavalry). Finally, during the Korean conflict, the Buffalo Soldiers were integrated into the rest of the army.

What became of Flipper after his court-martial? He left Fort Davis, migrated to El Paso, and worked in a laundry for a while. Then he became a civil engineer in the Southwest and Mexico. He became an expert on Mexican land law and wrote a number of books on the subject. In later years, he worked in the Interior Department in Washington, D.C., helped develop the Alaskan railroad system, and worked in the Venezuelan oil fields as an engineer. On nine occasions, he attempted to clear his name, but each time to no avail. He died in Atlanta, Georgia, in 1940, a broken and disheartened man.

During the 1970s, others interested in the Henry Flipper story tried to get his verdict overturned. Finally, on December 13, 1976, his dishonorable discharge was rescinded, and an honorable discharge was issued instead.

THE GREAT RAINMAKING EXPERIMENT

- 1891 -

EARLY ON THE MORNING OF FRIDAY, October 16, 1891, several curious onlookers gathered in Duval County, Texas, about one and a half miles from the San Diego railroad station. The site had recently been dubbed Camp Edward Powers in honor of the man who wrote the book, *War and Weather.* Published in 1871, the book strongly suggested that bombarding the atmosphere with loud explosions could force rain to fall "out of season." To support this bizarre theory, the author pointed to the downpours that sometimes followed the heavy use of artillery on the battlefield.

Several years after the publication of Powers's book, the U.S. commissioner of patents, General Daniel Ruggles, along with Senator Charles B. Farwell of Illinois, persuaded Congress to appropriate nine-thousand dollars to the Department of Agriculture to experiment with rainmaking. In mid-1891, a party of scientists gathered in Midland, Texas, to test the explosion theory. When a local newspaper reporter asked for an explanation of the theory, he was told:

*There are various currents of air passing through space
and when these become mixed or in violent contact a
storm is produced. It has been proved by many battles
that rain follows violent explosions. We are putting this
knowledge to test, and find that by our explosions on
the ground and one in mid-air we can cause a disturbance among the various air currents which, throwing
out moisture and heat, collect clouds.*

After the Midland experiment, none of the original appropria-
tion remained with which to continue the project. However, the
apparent success of the experiment encouraged local farmers and
ranchers to support the scientists' efforts. When Robert Kleberg,
foreman of the King Ranch, and his neighbor, N. G. Collins, pro-
posed that the scientists solicit private donations in the Corpus
Christi area, their suggestion was greeted enthusiastically. On September 24, rain continued for several days after an experiment near
Corpus Christi. Now, in October, scientists were conducting an even
more ambitious experiment at Camp Edward Powers.

On the day before the Duval County test was to take place, the
scientists had received a weather report stating that the entire region
would remain hot and dry as most of South Texas had been for many
weeks. Professor John T. Ellis of Oberlin College considered this a
perfect time to move ahead with his experiment. He informed his
associates that a series of explosions would be triggered during the
next two days and nights, some of them at ground level, some from
balloons, and some from a twelve-pound cannon that Kleberg had
brought from the King Ranch.

The explosives were made from a combination of dynamite and
a substance called rackarock. The ten-foot balloons were made of

muslin, covered with varnish, and filled with a mixture of oxygen and hydrogen. The professor planned to detonate explosives every five to ten minutes for several hours and then follow up with a more concentrated burst of nearly one thousand explosions on the night of October 17. The experiment was completed during the wee hours of October 18, at which time the sky was clear and star-filled.

At about three o'clock on the morning of October 18, clouds began to mushroom over the region. The wind suddenly changed direction, and it began to rain. Nearly half an inch fell by five o'clock in the morning. An hour later, the skies cleared again.

Most of the people of Duval County considered the rainmaking experiment an overwhelming success. One of the most vocal in his praise for the project was G. W. Fulton Jr. of Gregory, who had donated $300 to the effort. In a letter to Professor Ellis, he declared:

> *I have much pleasure in expressing to you my firm conviction that the San Diego experiment was a success. . . . I had promised myself the pleasure of witnessing it, and very much regret that pressing business called me to Victoria while the experiment was in progress. . . . At that time I was much discouraged, for I never saw less appearance of rain indications. I remarked to some of my friends that I was afraid the experiment was a flat failure, and on Monday morning following, when informed . . . that a half inch of rain had actually fallen at San Diego and over a wide area contiguous to that point, I was much surprised and gratified. . . . There were many people who attributed the rainfall to the intermingling of the cooler north wind, which arose*

Sunday morning, with the warmer moist air, losing
sight of several important facts. First . . . the rainfall
was before the norther and ceased after the norther
arose; second, the air was not moist. . . . And last,
but not least, there was no rain at all immediately
on the coast.

Since 1891, atmospheric scientists have learned a great deal about rainmaking, not least of which is the fact that noisy explosions will not produce rain. The Duval County experiment, it seemed, had been nothing more than a coincidence. But to the farmers and ranchers of South Texas, it was an overwhelming success.

SARAH BERNHARDT GOES ON TOUR

- 1892 -

THEATERGOERS IN DALLAS WOULD LONG REMEMBER February 2, 1892. For on that evening, the popular European actress, Sarah Bernhardt, performed on a local stage. The forty-seven-year-old performer had arrived in Dallas two days earlier aboard a special railroad car that sported brass ornaments on its walls and luxurious animal skins on its floors.

Bernhardt was decked in a Nile-green robe of silk and accompanied by her Saint Bernard and a tropical parrot. Behind her personal coach was a second car loaded to the brim with nearly 150 trunks of costumes, the sets for the various plays in which she was to appear, and four personal servants to attend to her every whim.

Although the audience at the February 2 performance seemed to enjoy it, a newspaper reporter was more skeptical. Was Texas really ready for Sarah Bernhardt? He wrote:

French play, spoken in French, and by French men and women. How many in the audience understood it? It is easier to say how many did not understand the words. But everybody who paid attention could interpret the gestures, facial expressions, and stage business. The people sat in the height of expectancy, waiting for the curtain to rise. When it rose . . . such a silence—and all attention. When will Sarah "come out?" This kept alive the people.

In the middle of the first act, she came, hat, bouquet, elegant toggery and all. It was Sarah. And she looked as natty and talked as glibly as you have heard of. Bernhardt of Paris, France, stood there and talked for good life. She talked French. So fast did she go it that French scholars could catch only a few words; and when Sarah uttered the word "mustache" a fellow sitting behind this reporter said: "Mustache; I got that."

A few days later Bernhardt moved on to Galveston, where she took some time off to go hunting. When she returned to town with thirty game birds, she remarked to the ever-present press corps, "Galveston is a beautiful place, and bird-hunting is very good." Before she left the Gulf Coast, she gave several stellar performances, causing the local newspaper to gush, "Rapturous Bernhardt Completely Captured the Intelligence of the Island City."

Among Bernhardt's hallmarks were the infinite variety and beauty of her costumes. This was not lost on a Galveston reporter who described one of the "magnificent" costumes as "a veritable work of art" that "almost baffles description."

Fourteen years after her first tour of Texas, Bernhardt returned to the Lone Star State for another series of performances. By now her entourage had grown so much that it filled a sleeper car, three coaches, and three baggage cars. In addition to the other actors who traveled with Bernhardt, there was her staff of two maids, two menservants, a masseuse, a private secretary, a special representative, and a man who took care of her three dogs.

On her second tour the popular actress ran into trouble with a national syndicate that held a monopoly on most of the country's theaters. Acts not sanctioned by the syndicate had a difficult time finding a hall in which to perform. Bernhardt's performances were among those not approved by the syndicate. As a result she was forced to perform in a tent. And so it was that on the evening of March 26, 1906, at Cycle Park in Dallas, Bernhardt appeared before five thousand eager spectators inside her own specially made tent, which she fondly called "La Place Bernhardt."

From Dallas, Bernhardt traveled to Waco and then to Austin, where three hours of constant rain had converted the grounds on which the tent had been erected into a quagmire. At that point, the manager of the Hancock Opera House opened his doors to the divine Sarah—in spite of the syndicate's sanctions.

Before the evening's performance, Bernhardt visited Governor S. W. T. Lanham and members of the Texas legislature. All official business was suspended while the politicians welcomed the actress, prompting a Waco newspaper editor to smirk, "Solons at Austin Fell Over One Another to Pay Her Homage."

Bernhardt went from Austin to San Antonio to Houston before giving her final performance at Tyler. Although she announced that her circuit of Texas represented her "farewell American tour," Bernhardt did eventually return to the United States, though not to Texas. In 1917 the seventy-two-year-old actress performed with only one leg, as the other had been amputated two years earlier due to an old injury. The divine Sarah continued to bring her audiences to their feet, just as she had in Texas years earlier.

THE MURDER OF A NEWSPAPERMAN

- 1898 -

WILLIAM COWPER BRANN WAS UNUSUALLY HAPPY THIS MORNING. It was April 1, 1898, and he was busy planning a much-needed vacation with his wife of twenty-one years, Carrie. It had been only six weeks since the U.S. battleship *Maine* had been sabotaged in Havana Harbor, and the Waco newspaper that Brann owned and operated, the *Iconoclast,* had been working overtime trying to keep its readership abreast of all the late-breaking news. In less than a month—although Brann would never live to see it—the United States would declare war on Spain and send a military force to Cuba in retaliation for the *Maine's* destruction.

Brann pushed himself away from his roll-top desk and rose from his wooden swivel chair. He buttoned his jacket, straightened his bow tie, and took his hat from the hall tree that stood nearby. Signaling one of his employees to join him, he left the newspaper office and headed down the street to dine at a local saloon on Austin Avenue, one of Waco's main thoroughfares.

After lunching and discussing the next issue of the newspaper, Brann and his associate left the saloon and started back to work. As the pair walked down Austin Avenue, they heard a gunshot. Brann felt an intense, burning pain in his back and turned around to see a man with a pistol step back into a doorway about ten feet away. Brann feverishly dug into his coat pocket, retrieved his own revolver, and emptied it into his assailant. The stranger fired several more times, each bullet finding its mark. After Brann fired his last round, he dropped to the sidewalk, dying. His bewildered friend watched as the attacker fell to the ground as well, mortally wounded by four of Brann's bullets.

Shortly after Brann was carried home for medical treatment, police identified the assailant as Tom E. Davis. A little investigative work showed that Davis was a political conservative—the opposite of Brann—and that he had strong ties with the nearby Baptist-run Baylor College. Authorities could only speculate, but they assumed that Davis's murderous act was somehow linked to an incident that had occurred three years earlier. In the pages of the *Iconoclast,* Brann had violently attacked Baylor for being so sanctimonious.

In 1895 Brann had learned that a fourteen-year-old Baylor student from Brazil was about to have an illegitimate child fathered by the brother-in-law of Baylor's president. The newspaper editor was only too happy to jump into the controversy and belittle Baylor's image, gleefully admitting that he took great pleasure in exposing such "social ulcers and special sectarian scandals" to his readership.

A couple of years after the Baylor reproach, Brann was almost killed when several thugs kidnapped him, severely beat him, and forced him to sign a confession retracting his attack on Baylor. The editor had hardly recovered from those wounds when a disgruntled Waco resident horsewhipped him on a downtown street. But the two attacks failed to slow Brann, who weeks later wrote in his newspaper:

*My Baptist brethren desired to send me as a missionary
to foreign lands, and their invitation was so urgent,
their expressions of regard so fervent, that I am now
wearing my head in a sling and trying to write with
my left hand. I'm too slight for a slugger . . . but I can
make a shotgun sing "Come to Christ."*

If Brann had been a typical newspaperman, the shabby treatment he seemed to attract might have been unusual. But most of his peers didn't consider Brann typical. He went a step beyond simply reporting the news. He specialized in name-calling, invective, and vituperation. Neither individuals nor institutions were spared Brann's poison pen, and when he joined a crusade for or against someone or something, it was usually with a vengeance. Once, when describing a New York socialite, he wrote:

*Mrs. Bradley-Martin does not exactly "look every inch
a queen," her horizontal having developed at the
expense of her perpendicular, suggesting the rather
robust physique of her father's beer barrels. Still, she is
an attractive woman, having the ruddy complexion of
an unlicked postage stamp and the go-as-you-please fea-
tures of a Turkish carpet.*

Brann took politicians and the federal government to task as well. In an article dealing with the quality of America's national leaders, he wrote:

*We have fallen into the bad habit of making the
U.S. Senate an old folks' refuge or asylum for senility,*

sending to the lower House of Congress pettifogging
attorneys who cannot pick up a livelihood by practic-
ing in chicken courts, then accepting for President
whatsoever chump is most satisfactory to the pluto-
crats. It is small wonder that, with such a captain
and crew, the ship of state is drifting to the devil. It
is small wonder that her precious cargo is appropri-
ated by pirates, that capitol and White House are
permeated by Wall Street's subtle perfume.

The day after Davis's attack on Brann, the newspaperman died at his home in Waco. Many of his ninety thousand subscribers were shocked, but others were not surprised by his murder. The man described as "a master of invective" by journalist H. L. Mencken, a pithy writer himself, had penned his last insult and censured his last victim. No more would he—as he, himself, once bragged—"hurl the cowardly and unclean curs to the profoundest depth of hell."

THE GREAT GALVESTON HURRICANE

- 1900 -

FOR THE PAST TWENTY-FOUR HOURS, Isaac M. Cline, the forecaster in charge of the Galveston weather station, had been watching the barometer closely. It was Friday, September 7, 1900, and beginning with an abnormal reading of 29.974 the previous morning, the mercury in the instrument had been dropping steadily. Now, this morning, the barometer registered 29.678.

On Thursday Cline had noted in his log that the weather was unusually hot for this time of the year, with the temperature peaking at 90.9 degrees Fahrenheit. On Friday the weather station would record a high of 91.1 degrees Fahrenheit. The forecaster knew that these were the kinds of conditions that gave birth to hurricanes. But the sky was fairly clear, except for some high-flying stratocumulus clouds, and the wind registered between ten and twenty miles an hour, from the north. According to Cline's later report,

The usual signs heralding the approach of hurricanes
were not present. A brick dust sky was not in evidence.

*This feature, distinctly observed in other storms in this
section, was carefully watched for.*

When Cline and his brother, Joseph, a weather observer working
in the same office, reported for work early on Saturday, September 8,
they read with interest an item that appeared in the morning newspaper. According to the article, "a terrific storm is now raging on the
Louisiana and Mississippi gulf coast. Great damage has been done to
shipping, but owing to the prostration of the wires, no details are
obtainable."

A second article also caught the Clines' attention. Filed just
before the newspaper went to press early Saturday morning, it read:

*"At midnight [Friday] the moon was shining brightly and the sky
was not as threatening as earlier in the night. The weather bureau had
no late advices as to the storm's movements and it may be that the tropical disturbance has changed its course or spent its force before reaching
Texas."*

But by the time Galveston residents had read the September 8
morning news, weather conditions had changed dramatically. At
7:00 a.m., when the Clines collected the morning weather statistics,
the sky was cloudy, the wind was up to twenty-three miles an hour,
and the barometer was continuing to fall. By 7:45, a steady rain had
begun. Although Isaac suspected that a severe hurricane was immi-
nent, he could not have known that within hours the most destruc-
tive storm in North American history would hit Galveston.

Anticipating a nasty storm and high tides, Isaac had already
begun to warn Galveston residents who lived nearest the Gulf of
Mexico to prepare for the worst. By 6:30 a.m., the forecaster had
wired his concern to the central weather bureau in Washington, D.C.

The telegram read: "Unusually heavy swells from the southeast, intervals one to five minutes, overflowing low places south portion of city three to four blocks from beach. Such high water with opposing winds never observed previously."

Throughout the morning, the angry gulf continued to lash the southern part of Galveston—the city's primary residential section. The business district, with its sturdier brick structures, was somewhat protected from the oncoming storm by the shield of houses that lay between it and the gulf. The wind velocity continued to increase, and at 5:15 p.m., the weather station's instruments on top of the Levy Building blew away. The Cline brothers could only guess at wind speed after that, but they later reported it reached at least 120 miles an hour during the worst part of the storm. Although the weather station's rain gauge had been destroyed early in the storm, later estimates suggest that at least ten inches of rain fell on Galveston on September 8.

Six thousand residents of Galveston were killed in the great hurricane of 1900. Isaac, along with his wife, three daughters, and brother Joseph, who had fought his way through flooded streets to their frame house at around 5:00 p.m., on Saturday, were inside the home when it was washed from its foundations and carried into the Gulf of Mexico. Miraculously, all of the family survived the harrowing ordeal—except for Isaac's wife.

Most of the residential section of Galveston was destroyed in the storm, while most of the business district was spared. General Thomas Scurry, commander of the Texas National Guard, which was dispatched to the city to prevent looting, summed up the situation like this:

> *Galveston has passed through an ordeal of wind and*
> *water, of wreck, ruin, desolation, and woe seldom if*

ever known in the history of the world. In the twinkling of an eye its homes have been demolished, its industries crippled, at least one-seventh of its population killed, and more than 15,000 of its surviving citizens made absolutely destitute. From a condition of splendid wealth it has been reduced to absolute poverty. Three-fourths of its estimated valuation has been totally destroyed. Two weeks ago there was but one city in America—Providence, Rhode Island—wealthier in proportion to its population. Today, there is scarcely a city in America poorer than Galveston.

Within hours the fourth-largest city in Texas had been reduced to a pile of rubble. Property damage in today's terms ran into the hundreds of millions of dollars. But out of tragedy sometimes comes triumph. City fathers vowed that their town would never again suffer such destruction. They passed ordinances requiring that all of Galveston Island be elevated several feet by importing millions of tons of sand and gravel. Many places in the downtown area were raised as much as seventeen feet. A modern sea wall was built that would protect the city in the future from abnormal tides.

A GUSHER AT SPINDLETOP

- 1901 -

Tendrils of smoke rose from the chimneys of Beaumont, Texas, on January 10, 1901, as the town's nine thousand residents braced for another frigid day. Otherwise the morning sky was clear and watery blue, but it wouldn't remain so for long.

Four miles south of town, Curt Hamill was lowering more pipe into the oil well he and his brothers had been drilling on a little knob of land known as Spindletop. They had bored through layers of quicksand and 140 feet of solid rock to reach their present depth of 1,020 feet. Yet still there had been no sign of oil.

Suddenly, a geyser of mud spurted from the black hole, drenching Hamill and the two men working beside him. The three scrambled for safety as six tons of four-inch pipe exploded from the derrick and fell like giant toothpicks over the camp. For a moment, all was silent. Then, with a roar like a cannon shot, a great plume of oil erupted from the well and spouted more than a hundred feet into the sky.

In town, the sound of the explosion rumbled through the streets, shaking windows, stampeding cows, and frightening the horses tied to hitching posts. Captain Anthony F. Lucas looked up from his shopping with a start. Had there been an accident at his oil well? he wondered. A frantic phone call from his wife only alarmed him more.

"Hurry, Anthony, something awful has happened," she reportedly cried. "The well is spouting!"

Lucas fled from the store, jumped into his buggy, and whipped his horses into a gallop. As he neared Spindletop, he saw a dripping, black apparition racing to meet him. It was Al Hamill, another member of the drilling team, and he had news that was to revolutionize the American way of life.

"Oil, Captain!" he shouted. "Oil, every drop of it!"

Before Spindletop, most of the oil produced in the United States had come from wells east of the Mississippi River. The largest of these yielded six thousand barrels a day—a mere puddle compared to the seventy to one hundred thousand barrels that Lucas's well would produce. It was Spindletop that inspired the term *gusher,* and it ushered in a new era of human progress—the age of liquid fuel. It also silenced those who had scoffed at the idea of significant oil fields in the West, including an official with Standard Oil Company who had once boasted that he could drink all the oil there was west of the Mississippi.

A fountainhead of doubt had nearly prevented the discovery of oil at Spindletop. A one-armed, former lumberman named Pattillo Higgins had been the first to believe that "black gold" flowed under the little hill in southeastern Texas. In 1892 he persuaded some of Beaumont's most prominent citizens to finance exploratory drilling. When three shallow wells yielded nothing but mud, the investors bailed out. To attract new ones, Higgins resorted to advertising in a magazine.

The only person to answer the ad was Lucas, an Austrian immigrant who was mining salt in Louisiana at the time. On the basis of his experience, he considered Spindletop a likely place to find oil. So he moved to Beaumont, and with the financial backing of a pair of Pittsburgh oil prospectors, he hired the Hamills and began to drill.

The resulting gusher far exceeded even Lucas's expectations. In his excitement, he hugged every man on the job. He stood in the inky rain, feeling, smelling, and tasting it to be sure he wasn't dreaming. Hundreds of people began converging on the hill—on foot, horseback, and bicycle, in wagons and in buggies. They were merely the first wave of an onslaught of fortune and curiosity seekers. One farmer watched the geyser for a few minutes, mounted his oil-drenched horse, and rode like Paul Revere through the streets of Beaumont shouting, "Oil! Oil on the hill!" By morning the momentous news had spread throughout the world.

The original well at Spindletop increased oil production in the United States by 50 percent and world production by 20 percent. And it was just a beginning. By 1902, four hundred wells had been drilled on the little dome, and more than a hundred oil companies had been formed to drill, produce, refine, and market Spindletop oil. Now that petroleum was available in such huge quantities, it became an inexpensive fuel. It was also lighter and more efficient than wood and coal. Soon automobiles were being fitted with engines fueled by gasoline, the most important product of crude oil. Steamships and locomotives converted from coal to oil. The Southern Pacific Railroad, the first large-scale user, announced that it saved $5 million in one year by making the switch. Soon petroleum was being used to heat homes and fuel factories and power plants.

In his book, *Road to Spindletop: Economic Change in Texas, 1875-1901,* John S. Spratt described the impact of the new flood of oil:

By 1904, at least 1,500 tank cars had been built to
move Texas oil. . . . In and around the Beaumont area,
foundations had been laid for refineries, some of them
ultimately to be classed among the largest in the world.
A beginning had been made in burying in the bosom
of Texas prairies a veinlike network of pipelines
through which would flow hundreds of millions of bar-
rels of "liquid gold," or its refined products. . . . Texas
became the land of the "new rich."

In addition to touching off an industrial upheaval in Texas,
Spindletop oil burning in fireboxes and exploding in combustion
chambers revitalized the industrial world, revolutionized the whole
technique of agriculture, and stepped up the tempo of life for the
entire nation.

LANGTRY'S VISIT TO LANGTRY

- 1904 -

BEAUTIFUL LILLIE LANGTRY COULD NOT BELIEVE HER EYES when she stepped off the Southern Pacific train onto the railway platform at Langtry, Texas. A world-renowned actress, friend of King Edward VII of England, wife of Sir Hugo de Bathe, and breeder of fine race-horses in Suffolk, here she was visiting barren West Texas. She was greeted on the platform by the local justice of the peace, the post-master, the stationmaster, several cowboys, and "thirty or forty girls, all about fifteen or sixteen . . . and . . . announced en bloc as 'the young ladies of Langtry.' "

Lillie knew that the town had been named in her honor by Roy Bean, the infamous justice of the peace who, until his death the pre-vious year, had taken it upon himself to dispense his own harsh brand of justice throughout much of extreme West Texas. The crusty old judge had written Langtry on several occasions, professing his admi-ration for the popular British actress and practically begging her to visit him. She had never had the opportunity to do so until now, the summer of 1904—and now Judge Bean was dead.

Because of her train's brief stopover, Langtry was "regretfully unable to see the town proper, which lay across the line and some little distance from the tiny wooden shed with 'Langtry' written upon it." However, she did manage to visit the Jersey Lilly Saloon, also named in her honor (though the sign painter misspelled the name). It was here that Bean had held court. In her autobiography, *The Days I Knew*, published in 1922, Langtry described the saloon like this:

> *I found it a roughly built wooden two-story house, its entire front being shaded by a piazza, on which a chained monkey gambolled, the latter (installed when the saloon was built) bearing the name of "The Lily" in my honor. The interior of the "Ritz" of Langtry consisted of a long, narrow room, which comprised the entire ground floor, whence a ladder stair-case led to a sleeping-loft. One side of the room was given up to a bar, naturally the most important feature of the place, while stoutly made tables and a few benches occupied the vacant space. The tables showed plainly that they had been severely used, for they were slashed as if with bowie-knives, and on each was a well-thumbed deck of playing cards. It was here that Roy Bean, Justice of the Peace and self-styled "Law West of the Pecos River," used to hold court and administer justice.*

Although her whistle-stop tour allowed Langtry only about thirty minutes to meet the townspeople, she had enough time to learn much about old Roy Bean. In her book she mistakenly identified him as a native of Canada, but he was actually born in Kentucky around 1827. By the time he was twenty-five, he had migrated to California, where he operated a saloon. Eventually he moved to Mesilla, New Mexico, served with Texas troops there during an abortive attempt to take New Mexico for the Confederacy, and ended up in San Antonio, where he married and had four children.

In time Bean moved again, this time to the small town of Vinegaroon, west of the Pecos River. He renamed it "Langtry" in honor of a woman he had never met. There, he soon established himself as the final arbiter of justice in the strip of West Texas lying west of the Pecos River. With absolutely no legal background, he dispensed a brand of law that would make a modern judge cringe. Once, in 1896, after the state had outlawed boxing, Bean invited a pair of fighters, one of whom was the legendary Bob Fitzsimmons, to take part in a boxing match in Langtry. Townspeople circumvented the law by building a pontoon bridge to an island in the middle of the Rio Grande, which constituted the international boundary between the United States and Mexico. There, in no-man's land, Bean held the fight. Afterward, happy spectators trooped back across the bridge to drink beer at the Jersey Lilly.

Then there was the time a railroad section boss appeared in Bean's court, accused of murdering a Chinese laborer. Bean's only available law book was one published in 1856 dealing with California jurisdictions. After several days of testimony that clearly implicated the foreman, Bean took the matter under advisement, carefully reviewed his ancient California law book, and finally rendered his verdict:

> *The Court has been very patient in inquiring into this case. It is true that the defendant shot the Chinaman and killed him. It seems as if there ought to be some sort of punishment meted out, but there doesn't seem to*

be any provided for. What they don't know about Chi-
namen in California they don't know anywheres, yet
I've looked this book through and can't find any place
where it is named as an offense for a white man to kill
a Chinaman. So far as the feelings of this Court goes it
would be the greatest pleasure to hold the defendant for
murder, but the situation is not the fault of this Court.
Therefore the judgment of the Court is that the defen-
dant be discharged.

Bean was found unconscious on the floor of his beloved Jersey Lilly Saloon on March 19, 1903. He died soon afterward and was buried in the Del Rio, Texas, cemetery. As for Lillie Langtry, she reported in her autobiography that her trip "was a short visit, but an unforgettable one." As she said her farewells, townspeople offered her Bean's pet bear, but it broke its chain and ran away before it could be loaded onto the train. Instead, she ended up with Bean's revolver, which she later hung "in a place of honor" in her English home.

QUANAH PARKER COMES HOME

- 1907 -

ACCORDING TO COMANCHE TRADITION, each person should return to his birthplace at least once before he dies. So, in 1907, at the age of sixty-two, Quanah Parker prepared to make a pilgrimage to the land where he was born: a flower-filled valley in West Texas that had inspired his name. In the Comanche language, *kwaina* meant "fragrant" or "sweet-smelling." The aging chief would find that, even after all these years, the valley still fit the description.

Quanah's journey exemplified the clash of cultures that had shaped his life. With several of his friends, he left his reservation in what is now Oklahoma and traveled south in one of the new horseless carriages. When he reached the valley known as Laguna Sabinas, he donned traditional buckskin and moccasins. Carrying a rolled buffalo robe, a blanket, a long ceremonial pipe, and some tobacco, he retreated alone to a grove of oaks and maples on a hill overlooking a small salt lake.

For three days Quanah alternately sat and smoked or roamed the hillside, praying and reminiscing. Wistfully, he thought of his youth, when he and his people had ruled the Texas plains. He remembered hunting buffalo and stealing his enemies' horses. Then white settlers had overrun the land, and the Comanche way of life had changed forever. Fortunately for his people, Quanah had helped to ease them through the tough transition. One day he would be remembered as the last chief of the Comanches.

Quanah was born in 1845 to Peta Nocona, a Comanche chief, and Cynthia Ann Parker, the daughter of a white Texas settler. Nocona had raided the Parkers' settlement in 1836 and had taken nine-year-old Cynthia captive. The Comanches adopted the girl, and she adjusted to their way of life and grew up happily among them. Eventually she married her captor and became the mother of his three children. The only visible signs of Quanah's white heritage were his steel-blue eyes.

By the time of Quanah's birth, the Comanches had become one of the largest Indian tribes on the continent—about twenty thousand strong. They reigned over an enormous domain that covered much of Texas and parts of Kansas, Colorado, New Mexico, and Oklahoma. But white settlers had begun migrating to Texas in the 1820s, and it wasn't long before the two cultures clashed.

In 1860 a group of cavalrymen and Texas Rangers attacked Nocona's band while it was camped on the Pease River. Most of the men, including Quanah, were away hunting buffalo. The soldiers recaptured Cynthia and her baby daughter, Prairie Flower, and returned them to the Parkers despite Cynthia's resistance. She no longer could speak English and had forgotten white ways. Later, Quanah would learn that she made several attempts to escape and return to her adopted people. When Prairie Flower died of disease, Cynthia was overcome with grief and died, according to some accounts, of a broken heart.

By the time Quanah was fifteen, he was a strong and fearless youth. He was also alone. His father had died of an infected wound, his younger brother of a fever. So, with no family ties to bind him, Quanah left his father's band and joined the Quahadis, the fiercest of the Comanche tribes.

It wasn't long before Quanah was considered one of the fiercest of the fierce. Determined to drive the white men from their ancestral home, the Quahadis raided homesteads with a vengeance. Quanah fought with fanatic zeal, and he also displayed good sense. When a war party of Quahadis was ambushed by U.S. soldiers, resulting in the death of their chief, the band's elders appointed Quanah to take his place.

Cavalry Captain Robert Carter, a veteran Indian fighter, faced Quanah's ferocity firsthand one day when he and his troops barely fought off a Quahadi war party. He later described the young chief in his memoirs:

> *A large and powerfully built chief led the bunch on a coal-black racing pony. His heels nervously working in the animal's side, with six-shooter poised in the air, he seemed the incarnation of savage brutal joy. His face was smeared with black war paint, which gave his features a satanic look. A large cruel mouth added to his ferocious appearance. Bells jingled as he rode at head-long speed, followed by the leading warriors, all eager to outstrip him in the race.*

Carter blamed Quanah for "some of the foulest deeds ever recorded in the annals of Indian warfare."

In 1867 the U.S. government called a treaty council at Medicine Lodge Creek in Kansas, hoping to move the Southern Plains Indians onto a reservation and end the confrontations between white men and red. Under the treaty each Indian family was to receive a tract of land, which they would own as long as they cultivated it. The government also promised to provide schooling for the children and regular rations for the next thirty years.

A cholera epidemic had recently devastated the Comanches, so ten of their chiefs signed the treaty, hoping to sustain their weakened bands. But the proud Quahadis boycotted the council meeting. They continued to fight for their homeland, massacring settlers and burning homesteads.

In 1870 the U.S. government assigned Colonel Ranald S. Mackenzie to put an end to the Quahadi raids once and for all. In September 1871, he led his troops onto the Texas plains and discovered one of the Quahadi villages. Before the cavalry could attack, Quanah led a war party past the sentries and into Mackenzie's camp. The Comanches cut loose the soldiers' horses, and, ringing cowbells and flapping buffalo robes, stampeded the frightened steeds.

By 1874 the Comanches faced another threat to their existence. Buffalo hunters had swarmed into the Panhandle and begun slaughtering the Indians' basic food supply. Quanah could foresee the impact this would have on his people. So on June 26, he and seven hundred of his warriors attacked a hide hunter's base camp at Adobe Walls.

They hoped to surprise the men in their sleep, but a loud noise alerted the hunters. Armed with new heavy-caliber Sharps rifles, they fought off the warriors, inflicting many casualties.

The attack on Adobe Walls brought an ultimatum from the U.S. government: All Indians who did not move to the reservation by August 3 would be exterminated. Once again Mackenzie took the field, this time with six hundred troops. In September he attacked a large Indian encampment in Palo Duro Canyon, burning tipis and supplies and capturing more than a thousand horses. The colonel ordered his men to slaughter the mounts in order to deprive the Indians of the means to hunt buffalo. He wanted to give them no choice but to live on the reservation.

Merciless as it was, Mackenzie's strategy worked. Small bands of starving Comanches began to surrender to the army. Quanah held out for another year, but on June 2, 1875, he, too, rode onto the reservation at the head of his people. He was the last Comanche and the last Southern Plains Indian to admit defeat and give up.

Ironically, Quanah proved to be as great a leader in peace as he was in war. He recognized that cooperation and compromise were now the only way for the Comanches to survive, so he set aside his hatred and counseled his people to learn the white man's ways. With the help of a tutor, he learned to speak English, and he sometimes met with the Indian agent wearing a three-piece suit and derby hat. Eventually the government appointed him to the Court of Indian Offenses, a position he would hold for a decade. He also traveled to Washington, D.C., several times to lobby for Indian rights, and he even rode in Teddy Roosevelt's inaugural parade.

Quanah looked for opportunities to improve the lot of his people. When he noticed that Texas ranchers had to herd their longhorns to market along trails that led through the reservation, he got the Indian agent's permission to charge a dollar a head for the privilege of crossing. Later he leased pasturage to wealthy Texas stockmen, an arrangement that brought in thirty to fifty dollars a year for each of his people. Some said he was one of the wealthiest Indians in America. He was definitely the most powerful and respected Indian on the reservation, and the government recognized him as the principal chief of the Comanches.

Four years after Quanah made his pilgrimage to the land of his birth, he died of pneumonia on the reservation, but not before he could call his medicine man to speak Comanche words for his departing spirit. He was buried wearing traditional Indian dress.

In 1930 Congress approved a tall, granite tombstone for his grave site. It reads:

Resting Here Until Day Breaks
And Shadows Fall and Darkness
Disappears Is
Quanah Parker
Last Chief of the Comanches

THE LAST GOOD-BYES OF
BONNIE AND CLYDE

- 1934 -

FOUR MILES EAST OF DALLAS, beside a moonlit country road, twenty-three-year-old Bonnie Parker sat chatting with her mother. One by one she shared the latest snapshots that she and her partner, Clyde Barrow, had taken—pictures of the pair with their arms around each other, of Clyde posing with a grin beside a stolen car.

It was bizarre, this clandestine family reunion of May 6, 1934. It was also extremely dangerous. Law officers from Texas and surrounding states had been hunting Bonnie and Clyde for the past two years. Each time the Parkers and Barrows sneaked away from their Dallas homes to rendezvous with the outlaw pair, they risked leading officers directly to their quarry. The families had begged Bonnie and Clyde to flee to safety in Mexico, but Clyde reportedly replied, "Seeing you folks is all the pleasure Bonnie and I have left in the world."

The Parkers and Barrows knew that each reunion with the young fugitives might very well be the last. So each was tainted by grief—and by the shadow of impending death. Emma Parker would later recall how casually her daughter spoke of dying, "as calmly as if she were discussing going to the grocery store."

"Mama, when they kill us, don't let them take me to an undertaking parlor, will you," she remembered Bonnie asking. "Bring me home. . . . It's been so long since I was home."

On the night of May 6, Bonnie gave her mother a copy of a poem she had written. Mrs. Parker's eyes swam with tears as she read the final stanza:

> *Some day they'll go down together;*
> *And they'll bury them side by side;*
> *To few it'll be grief—*
> *To the law a relief—*
> *But it's death for Bonnie and Clyde.*

Later that night, the outlaws bade their families good-bye for what would turn out to be the last time. Only two weeks later, on May 23, Bonnie's prophecy would be fulfilled in a hail of bullets and a tidal wave of blood.

The 1930s are often referred to as the Lawless Decade. As Americans suffered from the bank failures and property foreclosures of the Great Depression, desperate men turned to desperate means to line their pockets and wallets. Headlines were filled with the deadly deeds of John Dillinger, Pretty Boy Floyd, Al Capone, Bugsy Siegel, and Lucky Luciano. But few gangsters of the time would be more legendary than Bonnie and Clyde.

Clyde Barrow met Bonnie Parker in January 1930 at the West Dallas home of a mutual friend. Clyde was "a likable boy, very handsome with his dark wavy hair, dancing brown eyes, and a dimple that popped out now and then when he smiled," Emma Parker later recalled. "He had what they call charm." He also already had a police record, having been arrested for stealing cars. Within two months he would be sentenced to prison on seven counts of burglary and theft.

Bonnie "was an adorable little thing," according to Clyde's sister, Nell, "more like a doll than a girl." In *The True Story of Bonnie and Clyde*, which Nell wrote along with Emma Parker, she fondly described her brother's partner:

> *She had yellow hair that kinked all over her head like a baby's, the loveliest skin I've ever seen without a blemish on it, a regular cupid's bow of a mouth, and blue, blue eyes. . . . She had dimples that showed constantly when she talked, and she was so tiny; she was only four feet, ten inches tall, and weighed between eighty-five and ninety pounds. . . . She was so full of the joy of living, she seemed to dance over the ground instead of walking. . . . She overlooked (Clyde's) past with a sympathy and compassion that is evident only when a woman loves a man with all her heart and soul. . . . As I look back over the past, I realize that Bonnie's key crime was that she loved Clyde Barrow.*

Bonnie proved her love for Clyde when she agreed to smuggle a gun to him in prison, enabling him to escape. Days later Clyde was arrested again, this time in Ohio, after robbing a dry cleaner and a railroad office. He was hustled back to the Texas State Penitentiary but was paroled two years later, in February 1932, for good behavior. He returned to Dallas and his sweetheart, Bonnie—and to a life of increasingly violent crime.

In April 1932, Clyde and a partner, Raymond Hamilton, robbed a jewelry store in Hillsboro, Texas. As the store owner knelt to open his safe, a gun discharged, the bullet ricocheted, and the owner slumped to the floor, dead. From then on, Clyde's sister said, "one thing led to another, each one getting Clyde in just a little deeper, till in his mind there wasn't a chance for him to do anything but go on as he did." He knew if he were captured, he would die in the electric chair.

Before the end of the year, Clyde would commit several robberies, numerous car thefts, four more murders, and a kidnapping—often with Bonnie at his side. She would later tell her mother, "I never dreamed what I was getting into, mama. I only meant to go and be with him a little while—just a few months out of a lifetime. . . . Long before I was ready to come back home, the way was blocked, and my name was chalked up with Clyde's."

At first the public actually admired the pair for the daring bank robberies they committed. Bank failures had resulted in poverty for all too many Americans, and some romantically imagined Bonnie and Clyde as Depression-era Robin Hoods. Newspapers glamorized the outlaws' exploits. Young boys thrilled to accounts of fast car chases and narrowly eluded ambushes.

But attitudes changed as the body count rose. By mid-1934, Bonnie, Clyde, and other members of "the Barrow gang" had gunned down a dozen people, most of them lawmen. Officers began to view their capture as a personal crusade.

After the fugitives' moonlit meeting with their families on May 6, Bonnie and Clyde holed up for a while at the quiet country home of Clyde's bootlegger uncle in Nacogdoches County, Texas. When someone alerted local lawmen to their presence, the pair slipped across the border into Louisiana with an associate, Henry Methvin. By now the law was hot on their trail, and their days were numbered.

In Shreveport the gang stopped at the Majestic Cafe, and

Methvin went inside to buy sandwiches and soft drinks for the three of them. Bonnie and Clyde waited in the car. When a patrolman drove by slowly and studied them suspiciously, the couple sped away, leaving their partner behind. Officers assumed the pair would try to rendezvous with Henry at his father's farm south of Gibsland, Louisiana. So six of them set up an ambush on the long, straight stretch of road that led to the Methvin farm.

Serendipitously for the lawmen, Henry's father, Irvin Methvin, came driving along that morning in his Model A Ford truck. The officers stopped him, handcuffed him to a tree out of earshot, and jacked up the front end of the truck. They removed a wheel to give the impression that the old man had a flat tire. They had baited the trap. Now they had only to wait.

Meanwhile, Bonnie and Clyde drove to a nearby town to do a little shopping. Bonnie bought a magazine and was engrossed in it as Clyde steered his car toward the place where the lawmen crouched in the bushes. Just as the officers had hoped, Clyde slowed to help Methvin, whose truck he recognized. Dallas County Deputy Ted Hinton, one of the men involved in the stakeout, described the blood bath that followed in his book, *Ambush: The Real Story of Bonnie and Clyde:*

> *Suddenly, [Deputy Bob] Alcorn's deep bellow, "HALT!"*
> *arouses him [Clyde]. Alongside him Bonnie screams,*
> *and I fire and everyone fires, and in the awful hell and*
> *noise Clyde is reaching for a weapon, and the wheels*
> *are digging into the gravel as he makes a start to get*
> *away. . . . [A] drumbeat of shells knives through the*
> *steel body of the car, and glass is shattering. For a fleet-*
> *ing instant, the car seems to melt and hang in a kind*

of eerie and animated suspension, trying to move for-
ward, spitting gravel at the wheels, but unable to break
through the shield of withering fire. I see a weapon go
up; Clyde's head has popped backward, his face twisted
at the shock of pain as the bullets strike home. . . . My
ears are ringing. . . . I fire again at the sickening
bloody forms inside the car and rush to the driver's side
to grab the door handle where Clyde is slumped for-
ward, the back of his head a mat of blood. . . . I
scramble over the hood of the car and throw open the
door on Bonnie's side. . . . I see her falling out of the
opened door, a beautiful and petite young girl who is
soft and warm, with hair carefully fixed, and I smell a
light perfume against the burned-cordite smell of gun-
powder, and unreal smell of blood. . . . I cannot believe
that I do not really feel her breathing, but I look into
her face and I see that she is dead.

Someone would later count more than fifty bullet holes each in Clyde's and Bonnie's bodies. A total of 167 bullet holes pierced what would become known as "the Death Car," though some were probably made by the same bullets as they passed through both sides on the way in and out. Inside the car, officers found fourteen guns, about three thousand rounds of ammunition, and license plates from eight states. Beside these lay Clyde's saxophone and Bonnie's makeup case.

"The long chase was over," Emma Parker would later write. "The law had won. Bonnie and Clyde would never stand the world off again, two against death, for death had overtaken them at last."

THE ASSASSINATION OF A PRESIDENT

- 1963 -

THE TEMPERATURE WAS IN THE LOW SEVENTIES when President John F. Kennedy left his Fort Worth hotel on November 22, 1963, to stroll across the street and visit briefly with a waiting crowd. Earlier, clouds had threatened rain, but now, at 8:45 a.m., as Kennedy made his way across the street to a small park, the sun was trying to peek through. Mrs. Kennedy was not with her husband, and when an onlooker asked about her, the young president quipped that she "was busy organizing herself." He added, "It takes a little longer, but then she looks so much better than we do."

Although Kennedy's security people had warned him that Texas would not be the friendliest place for him to visit, they had been pleasantly surprised at the warm welcomes the president and his entourage had received in San Antonio, Houston, and now, Fort Worth. The crowd roared with laughter when the witty president told them of an occasion in France when he introduced himself as "the man who had accompanied Mrs. Kennedy to Paris." He added, "I'm getting somewhat that same sensation as I travel around Texas. Nobody wonders what [Vice President] Lyndon [Johnson] and I wear."

Returning to his hotel, President Kennedy spoke briefly to members of the Fort Worth Chamber of Commerce. Accompanying him were Mrs. Kennedy, Vice President and Mrs. Johnson, and Governor and Mrs. John Connally. After warning his audience that "this is a very dangerous and uncertain world," the president and his party were escorted to the airport, where Air Force One waited to transport them to Dallas.

As the plane taxied down the long runway at Love Field, thousands of spectators crowded the barricades to get a look at Kennedy. Hundreds of placards sported such slogans as, "Welcome to Dallas, J.F.K." and "Welcome Jack and Jackie to Big D." At 11:37 a.m., Air Force One pulled into Gate 28, and Kennedy and his retinue disembarked to the cheering of an eager crowd.

Thirteen minutes after touchdown, the Kennedy party had begun the eleven-mile journey to downtown Dallas. The motorcade's destination was the Trade Mart, where the president was to make yet another speech, this time on national defense. The Kennedys and the Connallys rode in the presidential limousine, which, because of the mild weather, had its bulletproof bubble top removed and windows rolled down. As the parade got under way, President and Mrs. Kennedy relaxed in the back seat and chatted with the Connallys in the front.

The motorcade crossed Dealey Plaza and turned left beside the Texas School Book Depository building. As it continued toward a series of underpasses, Mrs. Connally turned to the president and remarked, "You can't say that Dallas isn't friendly to you today."

Kennedy had barely opened his mouth to respond when the crack of a gunshot was heard behind the limousine. The president's head snapped backward, and he grabbed his neck. Governor Connally turned to see what the commotion was and was hit by a second bullet. A third hurled President Kennedy forward in his seat. Mrs. Kennedy screamed, "Jack! Oh, no! No!" as she reached for her husband.

As the motorcade sped toward a nearby hospital, news correspondents already were filing stories about the tragic event. Although facts were scarce, Merriman Smith, a member of the White House news staff, sent the following report over the teletype nine minutes after the shooting: "Kennedy seriously wounded perhaps seriously perhaps fatally by assassin's bullet."

Less than an hour later, President Kennedy was pronounced dead at Parkland Hospital. The chief surgeon told newsmen, "I am absolutely sure he never knew what hit him."

Meanwhile, lawmen, suspecting that the fatal shots had been fired from the Texas School Book Depository, searched the building and found a rifle, three empty cartridge cases, an empty pop bottle, and a lunch sack behind some cardboard cartons on the sixth floor. At 1:15 p.m., two miles from the murder scene, a Dallas policeman, J. D. Tippit, stopped a man who fit the description of the assassin. When the patrolman approached the suspect, the man pulled a pistol and shot Tippit three times, killing him instantly.

Thirty minutes later Dallas police were called to a movie theater to investigate a suspicious-looking individual who had ducked into the theater when a squad car approached. They arrested Lee Harvey Oswald after he tried to shoot at them with a .38-caliber pistol. Considering him their number-one suspect, they took him to police headquarters and booked him.

Less than an hour after Oswald's arrest, Vice President Lyndon B. Johnson took the presidential oath of office aboard Air Force One at Love Field. Beside him were a distraught Mrs. Kennedy and Mrs. Johnson. The plane carried back to Washington the body of the former president, along with the new chief executive, his wife, and Mrs. Kennedy.

The following day, as Kennedy's body lay in state in the East Room of the White House, police in Dallas built their case against Oswald. They found his fingerprints on the rifle found at the book depository and a receipt for the purchase of the rifle in his possession.

President Kennedy's body was carried to the Capitol on Sunday, November 24. Even as preparations were being made for services there, a frightening scene was taking place in Dallas. Local police were transferring Oswald from the city jail to the county jail when a man later identified as Jack Ruby leaped out of the shadows and shot Oswald once in the abdomen. Millions of viewers across the country watched the event on television. Ironically, Oswald died less than two hours later in the same hospital as his victim.

Within an hour of Oswald's murder, Dallas homicide officers closed the assassination case. But even today there are those who believe that the case was far more complex than it appeared and that it involved more than one lone gunman firing out the sixth-floor window of the Texas School Book Depository.

THE MARCH OF THE MELON PICKERS

- 1966 -

ON LABOR DAY 1966, THOUSANDS OF PEOPLE jammed the streets of Austin as they marched to the steps of the pink-granite statehouse. Waving signs and shouting slogans in Spanish, they were protesting the plight of migrant farm workers, some of the most exploited laborers in the nation. At their head plodded a burro named "Unoviente Veinticinco" ("1.25")—a symbol of the minimum wage the marchers were demanding and a reminder of the difference between men and beasts of burden.

The three-mile march down Congress Avenue was the climax of a protest that had begun three months earlier and almost five hundred miles away. In the lower Rio Grande Valley, farmers had long relied on seasonal workers—most of them Mexican Americans—to harvest their cantaloupes and other fruits and vegetables. Because a reservoir of cheap labor lay just across the Mexican border, these workers often earned only forty to eighty cents an hour for their backbreaking toil. Once described as "the forgotten men and women of the U.S. economy," they had none of the legal protections that other workers took for granted—no minimum wage, no ban on child labor, and no guarantee of the right to form unions.

Disgruntled Americans across the nation were on the march in 1966. Martin Luther King Jr. strode across the South, sowing his dream of civil rights for blacks. Youths marched on college campuses, protesting U.S. involvement in the Vietnam War. Women paraded through their communities, rebelling against the inequality of the sexes. And in the spring of 1966, César Chávez led striking California grape pickers to Sacramento to dramatize their demands for higher wages and better working conditions.

It was the success of Chávez's protest—which resulted in the creation of the United Farm Workers union and the adoption of a $1.40 state minimum wage—that inspired melon pickers in the Rio Grande Valley to strike the following June. When heavy rains ruined the Texas cantaloupe crop and caused the strike to fail, the workers decided to take their protest on the road. On July 4, about a hundred people began the dramatic trek to Austin. They planned to ask Governor John Connally to call a special session of the legislature to enact a $1.25 minimum wage for all Texas workers.

The march had the blessing of union and religious leaders, as well as the support of many liberal politicians. Its coordinators were Eugene Nelson, a union organizer and veteran of the grape pickers' strike; the Rev. James Novarro, a Baptist minister from Houston; and Father Antonio González, a Catholic priest in the Galveston-Houston diocese who got involved, he said, to promote "the dignity of man, justice, and a livable wage."

The number of participants waxed and waned as the march headed northward in the sweltering summer sun. Only ten hardy souls walked the entire route. Others demonstrated their support by marching with the farm workers for a few miles at a time. In late July a reporter for the liberal *Texas Observer* joined the protesters for two days and shared his impressions with readers:

> *It is the most appealing aspect of the Valley farm work-ers' march that a handful of unassuming, impoverished people normally given to civic passivity have, footstep by footstep along hot dusty Texas roads, created a feel-ing of both apprehension and elation among the onlookers of the region. . . .*
>
> *Farmers are about the only Anglos who appear dis-tressed by this wholly unforeseen but now widening rip-ple of protest that is making its way upstate. . . .*
>
> *I suppose, objectively, that marches are coming to be regarded matter-of-factly in the sixties, but subjec-tively the experience of this one is both exhilarating and exhausting. It's a world of blisters, dust, unrelent-ing sun, good conversation punctuated by periods of silent plodding—a world in which a drink of water becomes a luxury gratefully accepted. . . .*
>
> *The marchers alternated singing, in Spanish, "The Eyes of Texas" and "America," and shouting "Viva la justicia. . . ."*

On August 31, when the marchers were only forty miles from the capital, they received a surprise visit from Governor Connally and other state officials. The governor told the workers that, although they had marched peacefully almost five hundred miles to see him, he would not be in Austin to meet them on Labor Day because he didn't want to "lend the dignity, the prestige of my office to dramatize any particular march." He expressed his concern that marches elsewhere in the nation had occasionally turned violent and told them, "You don't need a march to come see me." He also said he would not call a special session of the legislature "because I don't think the urgency [of the wage problem] is of such a character that it has a compelling nature to it." The best he could do was to agree to favorably recommend action on a minimum-wage law at the next regular legislative session.

Though Connally's visit was demoralizing, marchers refused to let it dampen their enthusiasm and determination. They continued on to Austin and their jubilant Labor Day rally on the steps of the Capitol. The *Austin American-Statesman* estimated that ten thousand people attended what it called "the most outstanding demonstration by any minority group in recent Texas history."

And the *Texas Observer* editorialized: "The Valley farm workers' march to Austin was a triumphant event. The Mexican Americans of this state have now acted together with pride, dignity, and unity in a common social cause."

The passion created by the march of the migrant farm workers had far-reaching results. It did, indeed, prompt the 1969 Texas Legislature to pass a minimum-wage law that included agricultural workers. It also spawned what became known as the "Chicano Movement," or "El Movimiento," which helped to shatter other socioeconomic barriers faced by Mexican Americans in Texas.

BARBARA JORDAN TAKES HER SEAT

- 1967 -

WELL-WISHERS ALWAYS CONVERGE ON AUSTIN on the day new state legislators take their oaths of office. But the crowd that packed the statehouse on January 10, 1967, was larger than any the city had ever seen before. Hundreds of people had come by car and bus to be a part of that historic day. For the first time, an African-American woman would take a seat in the Texas senate.

Barbara Jordan had hoped that her arrival at the capitol would be a drama of modest proportions. "I didn't carry the American flag or go in singing 'We Shall Overcome,'" she later recalled. But her triumph meant almost as much to black Texans as it did to her, and they didn't intend to let it go unsung. As the representative from Houston made her way toward the Senate, wearing a white orchid on the bodice of her dress, she passed between two rows of smiling faces. As she entered the chamber, the throng in the gallery erupted into cheers.

"They didn't know about the rules [against disruptions by observers]," Jordan explained later. "I looked up at them and covered my lips with my index finger. They became quiet instantly, but continued to communicate their support by simply smiling."

While she waited to swear her oath in the rich, compelling voice that was to become her hallmark, Jordan scanned the gallery for her parents, sisters, aunt, and uncle. Later she asked her uncle in jest, "You didn't have any trouble picking me out down there, did you?"

For the next decade Jordan would play a conspicuous role in the politics of Texas and the nation. In 1972 she would become the first black woman elected to the U.S. Congress from the South and, in 1976, the first to deliver a keynote address at the Democratic National Convention.

But the role that propelled Jordan into the public spotlight was her membership on the House Judiciary Committee when it considered the impeachment of Richard Nixon. During televised hearings in 1974, she mesmerized the nation with an impassioned speech in which she denounced the president's Watergate abuses and reaffirmed her faith in the Constitution. She deftly used her race to help make her point:

> *"We, the people." It is a very eloquent beginning. But when that document was completed on the seventeenth of September in 1787, I was not included in that "We, the people." I felt somehow for many years that George Washington and Alexander Hamilton just left me out by mistake. But through the process of amendment, interpretation and court decisions, I have finally been included in "We, the people."*
>
> *Today I am an inquisitor. I believe hyperbole would not be fictional and would not overstate the*

*solemnness that I feel right now. My faith in the Con-
stitution is whole, it is complete, it is total. I am not
going to sit here and be an idle spectator to the
diminution, the subversion, the destruction of the
Constitution.*

*If the impeachment provision in the Constitution
of the United States will not reach the offenses charged
here, then perhaps that eighteenth-century Constitution
should be abandoned to a twentieth-century paper
shredder.*

The speech was so powerful that it prompted a friend of Jordan
to say, "I heard her on the radio, and I thought it was God."

Barbara Charline Jordan was born in a poor, all-black neighborhood in Houston on February 21, 1936—a time when schools were
segregated and blacks were expected to sit in the back of buses, eat in
separate restaurants, and drink from separate water fountains. She was
the youngest of three daughters of Benjamin and Arlyne Jordan. Her
father was a Baptist minister and strict disciplinarian. He didn't allow
his daughters to smoke, drink, dance, go to movies, or watch TV.

One of the greatest influences in Barbara's young life was her
grandfather, John Ed Patten. As a child she helped him with his junk
business, and he took the opportunity to offer this advice: "You just
trot your own horse and don't get into the same rut as everyone else."
In retrospect, it's obvious she took his words to heart.

"I never wanted to be run-of-the-mill," she once told a reporter.

Jordan decided while in high school that she wanted to be a
lawyer. She also joined the debate team and discovered that she had
a spellbinding voice that compelled people to listen to her. She won
medals for oratory on both state and national levels and continued to

hone her public-speaking skills after enrolling at Texas Southern University, an all-black school in Houston. She led the TSU debate team to a draw in competition against the prestigious Harvard team and later proudly noted, "When an all-black team ties Harvard, it wins."

It was while Jordan was at TSU, in 1954, that the U.S. Supreme Court ruled that black and white schools must be integrated. But to Jordan's frustration, change was slow in coming. "I woke to the necessity that someone had to push integration along," she later recalled. She decided to go into politics so she would be in a position to implement the desegregation laws.

After her graduation with high honors from TSU, Jordan attended law school at Boston University—one of two black women in a class of six hundred. Then, because she didn't have enough money to rent an office, she set up a private practice in her parents' kitchen.

Jordan's first experience with politics came in 1960, when she worked as a volunteer for the Kennedy-Johnson presidential campaign. From then on, she remained active in the Democratic Party, and in 1962, she decided to run for the Texas House. She lost, tried again two years later, and lost again.

"The public believed that a woman had to have, over and above and beyond other aspirations, a home and family," she later explained. "And any woman who didn't want that was considered something a little abnormal. . . . But I made the decision, and it was a fairly conscious one, that I couldn't have it both ways. And that politics was the most important thing to me."

In 1965 several legislative districts in Texas were reapportioned, and Jordan found herself in a new district with a large bloc of minority constituents. She decided to run for the state Senate, and this time she won by a landslide. Not only was she the first black woman ever elected to state office in Texas, but she was the first black member of the legislature since 1883. She was reelected in 1968.

Throughout Jordan's political career, she championed the rights of poor people and minorities. During her two terms in the state Senate, she helped to block a sales tax because she believed it would hurt the poor more than the rich. She cosponsored legislation establishing a state minimum wage and led the opposition to a bill intended to disenfranchise blacks and Hispanic Americans by tightening voter-registration requirements.

By 1970 the population of Texas had grown so much that it had earned another seat in Congress. Jordan decided to run for it, and she had the active support of her friend and mentor, Lyndon Johnson. She won by a landslide, garnering 80 percent of the vote. The former president also helped to get her an appointment to the House Judicial Committee—the platform that launched her to national prominence.

In 1975 the *Wall Street Journal* called Jordan a "comet in Congress" and said, "She is a very ambitious politician who uses her eloquence not only on behalf of high principles but also to get ahead. . . . [I]t isn't by hesitating that Rep. Jordan has achieved, in one congressional term, more honors and perhaps more power than most members of Congress can look forward to in a lifetime. . . ."

That same year, in a survey by *Cosmopolitan* magazine, seven hundred political-opinion leaders put her at the top of a list of women they most wanted to see become president.

Jordan was easily elected to a second term in Congress, and then a third. She was even mentioned as a vice-presidential candidate on the Carter ticket. But she missed Texas. In 1979 the University of Texas in Austin offered her a job teaching political ethics at the Lyndon B. Johnson School of Public Affairs. She took it, and her classes were so popular that the school had to hold a lottery to see which students could attend them.

In 1993 President Clinton appointed her chairwoman of the U.S. Commission on Immigration Reform.

Jordan died of pneumonia on January 17, 1996. She had recently been diagnosed with leukemia, and she had battled multiple sclerosis for several years. She spent the twilight of her life moving about in a wheelchair.

In an obituary published the day after her death, the *Houston Chronicle* summed up Jordan's life in a fitting epitaph: "With a will of iron and a voice of gold, she was one of the few black women to make a name in U.S. politics."

SHOWDOWN AT WACO

- 1993 -

BY MID-APRIL 1993, THE DAYS WERE GROWING WARM in Waco, and
when the sun arose on Monday, the nineteenth, a slight breeze blew
across the Branch Davidian compound at Mount Carmel. At a few
minutes past six o'clock, inhabitants of the small religious settlement
watched in horror as two U.S. Army M-60 tanks approached the
walls of some of the buildings and punched gaping holes into them,
at the same time inserting tear gas through the openings.

Within minutes, dozens of Bureau of Alcohol, Tobacco, and
Firearms (BATF) agents launched a small-arms assault on the compound, soon to be joined by four Army Bradley vehicles firing
forty-millimeter canisters of tear gas into the windows and the
holes pierced by the tanks. A voice could be heard over a public
address system that loudly declared, ". . . you have had your fifteen
minutes of fame. . . . Leave the building now. You are under arrest.
The standoff is over."

For the next six hours, the battle continued between the compound's residents, including many women and children, and the

federal government's assault team, which included members of the BATF, the Federal Bureau of Investigation (FBI), the U.S. Army, the Waco Police Department, the Texas Rangers, the McLennan County Sheriff's Department, the Texas National Guard, the Texas Department of Public Safety, and U.S. Customs.

At noon, as millions of Americans watched the proceedings in disbelief on national television, the compound's main building suddenly burst into flames. Within minutes the structure was totally destroyed. All of the people but nine who had cowered inside, fearing for their lives, were burned beyond recognition. At the end of the engagement when the final count was made, seventy-four Branch Davidians, including its self-proclaimed leader, thirty women, and twenty-one children under the age of fourteen, had been killed in the fiery battle.

Remarkably, the April affair was not the first confrontation between the Branch Davidians and federal agents. Some fifty days earlier, on February 28, at 9:00 a.m., seventy-six BATF agents, accompanied by a heavily armed vehicular convoy and two Blackhawk helicopters, assaulted the Mount Carmel compound under the pretense of conducting a "search and arrest" operation against the inhabitants for what the BATF termed "possession of illegal firearms materials and the possible illegal conversion of certain semi-automatic weapons into full-automatic ones." No one knows who fired the first shot, but when the battle was over, four BATF agents were dead and twenty wounded, while ten compound members were either killed or wounded.

The leader of the Mount Carmel Branch Davidians, an offshoot of the Seventh Day Adventist denomination, was a thirty-three-year-old native of Tyler named Vernon Howell, or, as he later became known to his followers, David Koresh. In the early 1980s Howell was dismissed from the rolls of the Adventist church in Tyler for causing discord among the membership and, by the summer of 1981, he had moved to Mount Carmel and embraced the membership there. He was a well-versed Biblical scholar who was quite sincere in his belief that he had been chosen to select followers who would assist in the ruling of the forthcoming Kingdom of God. He also believed that he was appointed by God to save as many earthlings as he could from the inferno that would accompany the end of the world as described in the Book of Revelation. By the late 1980s, Howell, now known as Koresh, took over control of the Mount Carmel membership.

Located on the prairie near the small village of Elk some nine miles east of Waco, the much more expansive religious commune that was originally housed on the site in the late 1950s counted nine hundred followers, nearly one thousand acres, a sizable dairy operation, nearly twenty residences, and several farm buildings. But by the 1990s, following a downturn in the order's popularity and its inability to maintain a steady increase in members, all of the land except seventy-seven acres had been sold, and the community provided home to less than 125 believers.

The background of the two raids now appears to gravitate around the federal government's interest in Koresh's gun dealings. During the summer of 1992, BATF agents had begun a preliminary investigation of the Branch Davidians, suspecting them of illegal firearms activities. Actually, the evidence suggests that Koresh's group was merely pursuing a strictly legitimate business in gun trading and selling, a business that had always been popular in Texas and the rest of the South and West. BATF agents had interviewed a local firearms dealer about their concerns and, when Koresh learned of the government's involvement in his personal affairs, he not only invited the investigators to Waco to discuss the issues, but also faxed copies of all of his gun purchase receipts to the local dealer for his review, along with his permission to share the receipts with authorities. Court records later showed that Koresh was on friendly terms, not only with the local sheriff but with other law enforcement officers and even a BATF agent who was working undercover and who had earlier attempted to infiltrate Koresh's organization.

When all the smoke cleared from the two government assaults, an entire Christian religious sect lay destroyed in Waco. Most of its members—including scores of women and innocent children—were killed and, therefore, can have no comment on the rightness or wrongness of the affair. The few survivors of the conflict were put on trial for a variety of felonies. When the verdicts came down, most of the defendants were found guilty of their various offenses and sentenced to from five to forty years in prison and fined upwards of ten thousand dollars each.

Much has been written about the tragedy that occurred at Mount Carmel. Government officials from Attorney General Janet Reno, who gave the orders to besiege the compound in April, all the way down to individual officers who were on-site at the time, have defended the brutal attacks as legitimate and within the legal authority of the federal government. Others—attorneys, private investigators, civil rights advocates, and religious leaders—are not so sure. In retrospect, it would seem that in its determination to prosecute what ended up being a minor infraction—if there was a legal violation at all—the federal government, as revealed in the testimony of some of its own operatives, botched this operation, taking the lives of eighty men, women, and children in the process.

TEXAS FACTS AND TRIVIA

Texas is the second-largest state in the nation after Alaska. It encompasses 266,807 square miles, or almost 171 million acres. The greatest east-to-west distance is about 756 miles, and the greatest north-to-south distance is about the same.

The name "Texas" is derived from the Caddo Indian word *taushas,* which means "friends."

The mean elevation of Texas is 1,700 feet. The highest point in the state is Guadalupe Peak in Culbertson County, with an altitude of 8,749 feet. The lowest point in the state (sea level) is along the Gulf of Mexico.

The geographical center of Texas is in McCulloch County, fifteen miles northeast of Brady.

The latest agricultural statistics (2002) show that Texas contains approximately 229,000 farms totaling about 130 million acres.

The 2000 census revealed that Texas had a population of 20,851,820 people, or 78 per square mile. The state ranks second in the nation for population behind California. The 2006 estimated population was 23,507,783.

The coldest temperature ever recorded in Texas was -23 degrees Fahrenheit on February 8, 1933, at Seminole. The hottest temperature was 120 degrees Fahrenheit on August 12, 1936, at Seymour and on June 28, 1994, at Monahans.

Texas became a republic after winning its independence from Mexico in March 1836. It became the twenty-eighth state of the Union on December 29, 1845.

Austin is the capital of Texas. Its population in 2003 was 672,011. Houston is the state's largest city with a 2003 population of 2,009,690. Other cities and their populations: Dallas, 1,006,877; San Antonio, 935,933; El Paso, 515,342; Fort Worth, 447,619; and Corpus Christi, 257,453.

Texas contains 254 counties.

The state motto is "Friendship."

The official nickname of Texas is "Lone Star State."

The state bird is the mockingbird (*Mimus polyglottos*).

The state flower is the bluebonnet (*Lupinus subcarnosus*).

The state gem is the topaz.

The state tree is the pecan (*Carya pecan*).

The state grass is sideoats grama (*Bouteloua curtipendula*).

The state dish is chili.

The state songs are "Texas, Our Texas" and "The Eyes of Texas."

The state flag consists of a white star inside a blue field along the flagstaff. The rest of the flag is divided horizontally into two equal parts: The top half being white and the bottom half is red.

BIBLIOGRAPHY

Books

Andrist, Ralph K. *The Long Death.* New York: The Macmillan Co., 1964.

Bannon, John Francis. *The Spanish Borderlands Frontier; 1513–1821.* New York: Holt, Rinehart and Winston, 1970.

Berlandier, Jean Louis. *The Indians of Texas in 1830.* Edited by John C. Ewers. Washington, D.C.: Smithsonian Institution Press, 1969.

Bolton, Herbert E. *The Spanish Borderlands.* New Haven: Yale University Press, 1921.

Botkin, B. A., ed. *A Treasury of Western Folklore.* New York: Wings Books, 1975.

Boyd, Eva Jolene. *Noble Brutes: Camels on the American Frontier.* Plano, Tex.: Republic of Texas Press, 1995.

Capps, Benjamin. *The Great Chiefs.* The Old West series. Alexandria, Va.: Time-Life Books, 1975.

Clark, James A., and Michel T. Halbouty. *Spindletop.* New York: Random House, 1952.

De León, Arnoldo. *Mexican Americans in Texas.* Arlington Heights, Ill.: Harlan Davidson, Inc., 1993.

Dockstader, Frederick J. *Great North American Indians.* New York: Von Nostrand Reinhold Co., 1977.

Earle, Jim. "Billy Dixon and the Mile-Long Shot," in *America: The Men and Their Guns That Made Her Great.* Los Angeles: Petersen Publishing Colo., 1981.

Englert, Steve. "Billy Dixon: Plainsman Supreme," in *1995 Dixie Gun Works Blackpowder Annual.* Union City, Tenn.: Pioneer Press, 1994.

Faust, Patricia L., ed. *Historical Times Illustrated Encyclopedia of the Civil War.* New York: Harper & Row, 1986.

Fehrenbach, T. R. *Lone Star: A History of Texas and the Texans.* New York: American Legacy Press, 1968. Reprinted 1983.

Four Days: The Historical Record of the Death of President Kennedy. United Press International and *American Heritage* Magazine, comp. New York: American Heritage Publishing Co., 1964.

Frantz, Joe B. *Texas: A Bicentennial History.* New York: W. W. Norton & Co., 1976.

Gillett, James B. *Six Years with the Texas Rangers.* New Haven: Yale University Press, 1925.

Goetzmann, William H., and Glyndwr Williams. *The Atlas of North American Exploration.* New York: Prentice Hall General Reference, 1992.

Haley, James L. *Texas, From Frontier to Spindletop.* New York: St. Martin's Press, 1985.

Hamill, Curtis G. *We Drilled Spindletop.* Houston, privately printed, 1957.

Haskins, James. *Barbara Jordan.* New York: Dial Press, 1977.

Hinton, Ted, as told to Larry Grove. *Ambush: The Real Story of Bonnie and Clyde.* Bryan, Tex.: Shoal Creek Publishers, 1979.

Jordan, Barbara, and Shelby Hearon. *Barbara Jordan: A Self-Portrait.* Garden City, N.Y.: Doubleday & Co., 1979.

Justice, Glenn. *Revolution on the Rio Grande.* El Paso: Texas Western Press, 1992.

Kendall, George Wilkins. *Narrative of the Texan-Santa Fe Expedition.* New York: Harper and Brothers, 1844.

Kissinger, Rosemary K. *Quanah Parker: Comanche Chief.* Gretna, La.: Pelican Publishing Co., 1991.

Lea, Tom. *The King Ranch.* Boston: Little, Brown and Co., 1957.

Lloyd, Everett. *Law West of the Pecos.* San Antonio: The Naylor Co., 1935.

Long, E. B., ed. *The Civil War Day by Day: An Almanac.* Garden City: Doubleday & Co., 1971.

Long, Jeff. *Duel of Eagles.* New York: William Morrow and Co., 1990.

Metz, Leon C. *Roadside History of Texas.* Missoula, Mont.: Mountain Press Publishing Colo., 1994.

———. *The Shooters.* El Paso: Mangan Books, 1976.

Myers, John Myer. *The Alamo.* Lincoln: University of Nebraska Press, 1973.

Nevin, David. *The Texans*. Alexandria, Va.: Time-Life Books, 1975.

Parker, Emma, and Nell Barrow Cowan. *The True Story of Bonnie and Clyde*. Compiled and edited by Jan I. Fortune. New York: New American Library, 1968. Originally published as *Fugitives: The Story of Clyde Barrow and Bonnie Parker*. Dallas: The Ranger Press, Inc., 1934.

Parkman, Francis. *La Salle and the Discovery of the Great West*. Williamstown, Mass.: Corner House Publishers, 1968.

Rister, Carl Coke. *Comanche Bondage*. Lincoln: University of Nebraska Press, 1989.

Robinson, Charles M., III. *Frontier Forts of Texas*. Houston: Lone Star Books, 1986.

Sauer, Carl Ortwin. *Sixteenth Century North America*. Berkeley: University of California Press, 1971.

Sonnichsen, C. L. *The El Paso Salt War of 1877*. El Paso: Texas Western Press, 1961.

Spratt, John S. *The Road to Spindletop: Economic Change in Texas, 1875-1901*. Dallas: Southern Methodist University Press, 1955.

Tabor, James D. and Eugene V. Gallagher. *Why Waco?* Berkeley: University of California Press, 1995.

Tanner, Ogden. *The Ranchers*. Alexandria, Va.: Time-Life Books, 1977.

Terrell, John Upton. *American Indian Almanac*. New York: The World Publishing Co., 1971.

Thrapp, Dan L. *Encyclopedia of Frontier Biography*. Glendale, Calif.: The Arthur H. Clark Co., 1988.

Tilghman, Zoe A. *Quanah: The Eagle of the Comanches*. Oklahoma City: Harlow Publishing, 1938.

Twice-Told Tales of Texas. Austin: Texas Memorial Museum, 1939.

Utley, Robert M. *The Indian Frontier and the American West; 1846-1890*. Albuquerque: University of New Mexico Press, 1984.

Utley, Robert M., and J. U. Salvant. *If These Walls Could Speak: Historic Forts of Texas*. Austin: University of Texas Press, 1985.

Walker, Dale L. *Mavericks—Ten Uncorralled Westerners*. Phoenix: Golden West Publishers, 1989.

Wallace, Edward S. *The Great Reconnaissance*. Boston: Little, Brown and Co., 1955.

Webb, Walter Prescott. *The Texas Rangers, A Century of Frontier Defense*. Austin: University of Texas Press, 1987.

Weems, John Edward. *Men Without Countries*. Boston: Houghton Mifflin Co., 1969.

Winegarten, Ruthe. *Black Texas Women*. Austin: University of Texas Press, 1995.

Wormington, Helen M. *Ancient Man in North America*. Denver: The Denver Museum of Natural History, 1957.

Other Sources

Austin American and American-Statesman, July 5, 1966; September 1-11, 1966.

Campbell, Randolph B. "The End of Slavery in Texas: A Research Note." *Southwestern Historical Quarterly*, July 1984.

Clines, Francis X. "Barbara Jordan Dies at 59; Her Voice Stirred the Nation." *New York Times,* January 18, 1996.

Dugan, Frank H. "The 1850 Affair of the Brownsville Separatists." *Southwestern Historical Quarterly,* October 1957.

Dugger, Ronnie. "A Long Struggle with La Casita." *Texas Observer,* June 24, 1966.

Everett, Donald E. "San Antonio Welcomes the 'Sunset'—1877." *Southwestern Historical Quarterly,* July 1961.

Hines, Cragg. "Barbara Jordan Lived as Pioneer and Prophet." *Houston Chronicle,* January 18, 1996.

King, C. Richard. "Sarah Bernhardt in Texas." *Southwestern Historical Quarterly,* October 1964.

McLean, Malcolm D. "Tenoxtitlan, Dream Capital of Texas." *Southwestern Historical Quarterly,* July 1966.

Maraniss, David. "Due Recognition and Reward." *The Washington Post Magazine,* January 20, 1991.

"The March: A Triumph, a Task." *Texas Observer,* September 16, 1966.

Nader, Albert J. (producer). *Dillinger, Capone, and Bonnie and Clyde.* Television documentary written by Nick Bougas and Toni Lavagnino and aired on The Learning Channel, February 1996.

Olds, Greg. "Two Days on the Road." *Texas Observer,* August 5, 1966.

———. "Labor Day in Austin: A Bad Day for the Establishment." *Texas Observer,* September 16, 1966.

Rayburn, John C. "The Rainmakers in Duval." *Southwestern Historical Quarterly,* July 1957.

Weems, John Edward. "The Galveston Storm of 1900." *Southwestern Historical Quarterly,* April 1958.

INDEX

INDEX

ABOUT THE AUTHOR

James A. Crutchfield is the author of forty books dealing with various aspects of American history. He is the author of eight titles in the popular "It Happened In . . . " series: Montana, Colorado, Washington, Oregon, Arizona, New Mexico, Texas, and Georgia. He has contributed hundreds of articles to newspapers, journals, and national magazines such as *The Magazine Antiques, Early American Life,* and *The American Cowboy.*

Crutchfield's writing achievements have been recognized with awards from the Western Writers of America, the American Association for State and Local History, and the Tennessee Revolutionary Bicentennial Commission. A former board member of the Tennessee Historical Society, he presently sits on the Board of National Scholars for President's Park in Williamsburg, Virginia. He and his wife, Regena, reside in a pre–Civil War home in Tennessee.

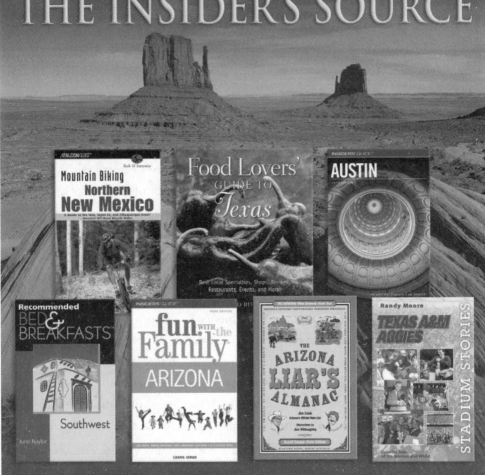